"Millionaire is the
New Middle Class."

GRANT CARDONE'S
PLAYBOOK

Grant Cardone Bio

Grant Cardone is a self-made entrepreneur who with no money, no connections, and no fancy degrees founded and operates privately held businesses that have sales of almost $100 million a year, real es tate holdings just shy of half a billion dollars, and has a personal net worth of nine figures.

Cardone is a New York Times best-selling author of five books, a nd over a dozen best-selling business programs and webinars. Grant was voted one of the top 5 CEO's in the world and is considered o ne of the top social media influencers on the Internet today.

In addition to his entrepreneurial commitments and family, he is h ighly active in philanthropic activities raising over $100 million last year for charities.

Grant Cardone's Playbook is the first compilation of notes from Gran t's best material on how to get rich all in one easy-to-use guide for your reference. Just as the great athletes use a playbook to study their plays and get game-ready, use this until you know the material by heart.

The better you know your Playbook, the more successful you'll be.

Note from Grant

It is my personal life mission to help you and as many other s as possible. I am blessed in having accomplished amaz ing financial success in my own life, and now I turn my a ttention to doing what I can to help others.

I am gravely concerned about the financial literacy and c ondition of those around me. Clearly most are operating w ith incorrect information and comprehension of the financ ial scene. You are being given lots of bad informati on everyday and it is my hope that this program straighten s out and simplifies the path for you.

Regardless of what condition you find yourself in at this time I assure you it can be improved. Please stay in touch w ith me and let me know of your successes.

I really do care about you,

G. Cardone

Contents

PERSONAL
FINANCES

Course
Personal Finances

Personal finances is **defined as the financial management which an individual or a family unit performs to budget, save, and spend monetary resources over time.** The most important thing missing from this definition is how to produce the finances in the first place.

If you never take responsibility for your personal finances you will never be in control of them. Most people have given up completely on them. **Most have given up because the information they have been operating with was not designed to get rich, but instead keep a person trapped.** Money and success demand attention. If you ignore either, you'll get neither. My wife and I look at our personal finances weekly. Most of these meetings are short and boring where we simply take a few moments to look at where we are, where we want to be and anything we need to clean up. Creating financial prosperity demands you take responsibility over your personal finances. You must look at them, pay attention to them and take control over them.

"If you don't pay attention to your personal finances someone else will."

Income is King

If you don't have new income you reduce your chances of creating wealth. Income is king and you must continue to focus on how to increase your income. I know this sounds basic—because it is—but a lot of people have this confused.

People spend time trying to save money prematurely or paying down debt when at the beginning stages of wealth building you should only focus on increasing income. Look, if you don't have income then there is no money to save, no money to retire, and no money to invest.

There is no chance of wealth without income first. You might hear people say, "Income is not what you want because it is taxed heavier than other more passive investments." Well that may be true but you won't have money to invest without income. You should never disparage the concept of a job or any vehicle which gives you the ability to produce income.

Now the question becomes, how much income can you create at the job or jobs you have? Then it will be how much can you incrementally increase your income at that same location.

Saving is not king, spending is not king. Income is KING. And that is the number one most basic building block you need. Yes, it is taxed at the highest rates but income is the first doorway to creating wealth.

Takeaways:
1) Income is King
2) Income should never be disparaged
3) Question is: How much income can you produce from one location?

Income Increments

You aren't going to go from 4K a month to millionaire. There must be incremental growth—this isn't a "get rich quick" deal. Now I'd certainly like to explode and go 10X but understand that there are going to be increments. At 25 years old, I was making 4K a month and all I could focus on was increments.

I thought about how I could take that 4K and control it by going up to $4,400. Could I increase it by 10%? That would be $400 more per month. That's $100 a week. Who do I need to see, who do I need to call? At 35 years old it wasn't going from $4,000 to $4,400 but going from $15,000 to $20,000. That doesn't mean I'm not thinking about how to explode with growth, but every day, every week I'm thinking about how to increase in increments.

Think about it this way—do you want more or less? There is no same. Same always falls to less. You'll get what you focus on. If you focus on anything else other than more, you'll get less. You'll end up with less money, less income, less ability to save and invest money.

Takeaways:
1) Keep going for small increases.
2) Acknowledge small wins along the way
3) Look for surges

95/5 Rule

Most people spend most of their time looking at what they spend rather than what they make. Your way out is through income, not reducing expenses. Certainly I don't want to spend more than I make. I want to make so much I can't spend it all. Now I know there are some people who would spend as much as they make no matter how much they make – they are unethical and irresponsible and dangerous people.

The rule for handling personal finances is spend 95% of your time and energy on income and five percent of your time and resources on your expenses. Take out your household income statement, hopefully you have one. It's a statement of your income and expenses. The lines for income are only a few and the entries for expenses are many. Income is so powerful that it only takes a few lines of income to exceed the many lines of expenses. The 95/5 rule suggest you spend most of your time on the income not the expenses. Most people have this in reverse—they spend most of their time on expenses and little time on income.

How much time do you spend on the income side? If you are anything like the average American, you are spending all of your time on the expenses and not enough time on the income. In your weekly meetings looking at your finances spend most of your time on income (the solution) not expenses.

Your target is to create enough income in the future to save 40% of your gross income. This will force you to increase your income to new levels. Most people are saving less than 5% of their income, never enough to create wealth. The supposed finance experts say you should have 3 months of savings because they don't believe in your ability to produce income. **Learn how to play offense and get more money and stop spending all your time on defense (saving money).**

Takeaway: Spend 95% of your time on income not expenses.

How to Use a Credit Card

While credit cards have gotten a bad reputation for late fees, penalties, and high interest rates, the informed person knows how to use credit cards. **All wealthy people have credit cards so the credit card itself is not the problem.** Wealthy people do not allow themselves to be used by the credit card companies they use the credit card companies.

Most people get a credit card because they have simply given up on their ability to get money. Reverse this by making your decision to only use credit cards to record all purchases and be a statement of your activity. I have never in my entire life paid interest or late fees for a credit card—I use them, they don't use me.

Pay off your balance in full each month and use them as accounting devices. I never keep receipts. I use the monthly statement provided by the credit card company. Your credit card tracks all your spending. You also rack up points that you can use on hotels, airline tickets, car rentals, etc. that you wouldn't get using cash.

Takeaways:
1) Use them don't let them use you
2) All wealthy people have credit cards.
3) Never pay interest, pay them off in full each month.

Good Debt vs. Bad Debt

Debt is defined as something owed or that is due.

You've been told don't use debt, never use debt, all debt is bad and some even suggest evil. But all debt is not created equal, some debt is bad and some is actually good. There are times when I want to owe others something and certainly times when I want others to owe me.

There's time to use debt and there's time not to. When do you use debt? Use debt when others pay for it and it helps you grow your business or enterprise. There's no 'always' in anything. Some of the greatest companies on this planet use debt to grow and scale their businesses.

Debt used to increase my ability to go into the marketplace and produce more income, not buy more things, is good debt. The rule is if debt can increase your income or make you better or get you known use it. The rule for bad debt is if you are using debt to consume, eat or entertain it is bad debt.

Not all debt is created equal. I use debt to build income. Debt is me going to the bank to borrow money to build my business. Look at Apple, they have $270 billion in cash and they borrow money.

I have over $300 million in debt in my real estate business. It is cheap money and allowed me to grow my business. This debt by the way is being paid down by the operations while I get the write-offs as a result.

Takeaways:
1) Not all debt is bad debt
2) Never use debt to consume
3) Debt used to increase income or make you better or better known is good debt.

Stay Broke

I mentioned earlier your goal is to save 40%. This is an extremely aggressive goal but one that history shows is how the wealthy operate. Check out the chart below where the top 1% save almost 40% of their income over the last 100 years allowing them to make big investments. **How can you save 40%? Make a lot of money!** And when you do get rid of that new made money and put it in sacred accounts that will leave you broke so you can prepare to invest.

When you have incremental increases or surges in income save it all by going broke and setting that money aside in special accounts until you are ready to invest. Never have money just sitting around. Money gets bored and when it does it gets wasted.

Staying broke doesn't mean you are poor it means you have made a commitment to putting new earned money aside so one day you can make big moves. I purposely make myself broke two or three times a year never allowing money to just sit around and I never increase my standard of living until I have new income from other streams I can depend on (more on this later.)

Takeaways:
1) The only way to save 40% of income is to make a lot of money
2) When you have incremental increases or surges save it all.
3) Money gets bored

Saving rates by wealth class (decennial averages)

The rich save more as a fraction of their income, except in the 1930s when there was large dis-saving through corporations. NB. The average private saving rate has been 9.6% over 1913-2013.

Source: Emmanuel Saez and Gabriel Zucman, The Distribution of U.S. Wealth, Capital

PERSONAL FINANCES

Shortage Mindset

If you were brought up poor or middle class like I was you are left with the beliefs and actions of the poor and the middle class. This becomes your shortage of money mindset.

You believe that there is a shortage of money so there is. There is more money on this planet than there are trees. You can print money faster than you can grow a tree. Money is everywhere and if you have a money shortage in your life right now it started in your mind.

"There is no shortage of money on this planet so if you have a shortage of money it's a problem with you not with money."

Go outside and look around for signs of wealth, prosperity and abundance. Cars, buildings, stores, the retail centers, and on and on. There is no shortage of money there are merely too many people who have a mental block on abundance.

If you were brought up poor or middle-class you were brought up by people that believed money was in shortage. "Turn the lights out, eat all your food, a penny saved is a penny earned" and all the little money confusions and falsities. Look, a penny earned is a PENNY. Fix this money shortage mindset and start paying attention to how much money there is in the world. See how much money is around you. If where you are is limited go where you can see abundance easily and admire it.

Takeaways:

1) There is no shortage of money
2) You believe in shortages so there are shortages
3) Go where you can see abundance easily and admire it.

Worried About Prices

You know the old saying that if you have to know the price you can't afford it? That's actually not true. The bigger issue is when you are constantly looking at prices, complaining about prices and worried about how much something cost you are not producing enough.

Your constant concern about the cost of something is a reminder you are not yet producing at your full potential. Why are you fixated on the price of something? Price is a way in which people deceive themselves from seeing value. Everyday people buy things they don't need because the price is so 'good' and yet they deprive themselves of the things they really need because the price is too high.

Price is not your problem. The price is not what you are buying. I did this for years—I'd go to a restaurant and look at the prices on the menu. Do you think the super wealthy worry about the price of a steak or a cup of coffee? Wealthy people don't worry over price, they produce more income than they can spend. They aren't worried over a $30 book or a $1000 program, their attention is focused on abundance and expansion.

The average American makes $52,000 a year where the average cost of living is higher than $52,000 a year. 76% of all Americans live paycheck to paycheck in the wealthiest country in the world. It's no different for a person in America than it is for a guy in India making $2 a day.

People focus on the wrong thing. All this attention on what things cost is a reminder of not producing enough. **Shift your attention away from price to production.** Looking at prices is an indication that you've contracted financially.

Takeaway: Stop thinking about costs and re-focus again on income.

TOP MONEY MISTAKES

PERSONAL FINANCES

Top Money Mistakes

Saving to Save

You've been told your entire life to save your money. It's impossible to create real wealth just saving. You can't show me a wealthy person that has ever gotten wealthy because they saved their money or because they are bargain hunters or clip coupons. Your mom and dad said save your money.

The wealthy don't get wealthy like that. They only had it half right. If you put your money in the bank you might get .25%—that's 40 years to earn 10% on your money. The banks don't pay anything today. Money that sits in the bank, or in your house, always seems to find an emergency to go fund. Dave Ramsey has said, "Do not carry cash or credit cards, because when either is available, you'll create a reason to use it." If you get more money in more money goes out. You get a pay raise you start spending more money.

That's why when I was 25 I started a sacred savings account where I parked my money so I couldn't touch it. How many old people do you know, 90 years-old who have a million dollars that they never even enjoyed? They never went all in to let their money grow to wealth where they felt they could really live life. They saved their whole life.

The only reason to save money is to one day invest it. Never save to save, save with the purpose of making a big play one day!

PERSONAL FINANCES

Top Money Mistakes

Pretender Spender

On the other end of the spectrum from the miser, the saver and the frugal is the pretender spender acting like a big shot who isn't. Trying to impress everyone by picking up dinner, flashing a big watch, and a convertible doesn't mean you have wealth. Real wealth doesn't roll like this. Most of the time it is an understated show of wealth.

A real player is not trying to impress people with sports cars, designer clothes, and VIP tables. The wealthy don't try and impress people they don't know, they are trying to one day live a life of freedom. They seek freedom not praise. The wealthy are not trying to say look at me and what I have got. And at the point when it does look like they are just throwing it around it's because they have so much they are now in a position to just waste it.

When the wealthy spend money on ridiculous things like cars, boats, planes, and homes, the truth is that no matter what poor investments they make they can afford to waste money. That is the freedom I'm talking about, when you can spend money like it doesn't matter. The fake baller is a middle class guy that is pretending to be wealthy when he/she is not, living beyond their means.

A wealthy display of extravagance is nothing compared to the discipline these people invested yesterday to create the wealth they have today. The money they are spending today is miniscule to the abundance of what they've created. Wealth provides you with options.

Top Money Mistakes

Comparing to Others

A common problem is thinking to yourself that you are better off than someone else. 76% of all working Americans live paycheck to paycheck who barely get by no matter how much money they make. I know people in the U.S. who compare themselves to people in 3rd World Countries. Never ever compare yourself to someone else's financial condition.

There's always someone worse off and there's always someone better off. You're better off than the homeless person and you're way worse than Warren Buffet.

Your income and wealth has nothing to do with mine and likewise. If you are better off than a homeless person that in no way helps you pay your bills, feed your children or take care of your parents. People constantly tell themselves, "but we are so much better off than...." This is a ridiculous analogy people make to give themselves a false sense of security.

Never compare yourself to another; it doesn't solve your problems.

PERSONAL FINANCES

Top Money Mistakes

Investing in Trends

Trend is defined as a general direction in which something is developing or changing or it can also mean a fashion.

I avoid investing in the latest trends and the next greatest thing and keep my game focused on my space and what I can do. Certainly I am always open to learning and reading and studying for the direction and developments. But I avoid trying to hit trends. By doing this I know I will pass up some huge hit, some home run grand-slam investment. I am sure I have missed many great opportunities—but while I was missing the big trend I was able to go all in on the things I knew were not just trends.

Warren Buffett invest in electricity, railroads, banks, insurance, soft drinks, candy—but he swore he'd never invest in technology until he bought into IBM.

Do not get lured in by the latest greatest hottest technology that comes today and where most is gone tomorrow—and very few change the world forever. Don't get on the rollercoaster ride of maybes and things you don't know. **Where there is uncertainty, there will be losses.** Seek situations that guarantee the arrival of wealth; they are out there.

PERSONAL FINANCES

Top Money Mistakes

Trusting Without Proof

The single biggest financial mistake I've made was naively trusting people because I liked them and because it felt right without proof. **If you can't ask someone to validate what they are telling you don't do business with them.** Of everything they presented—their financial condition, how the company was doing—I failed to get proof. Instead, I went with feelings and I was deceived. By the time I had figured out I had been deceived, I was out millions of dollars.

Disregard your feelings when it comes to trusting others and demand validation. If you can't ask someone for solid evidence, if you feel so good about the people that you can't say, "show me", show me your bank statement, show me where you made that money, show me that exact number that you just stated, if you can't ask those questions—don't go into business with them. People betray other people, it happens.

Show me don't tell me is my mantra.

If you can't show me that says enough to me.

If I can't ask you, then we can't go there.

Top Money Mistakes

Seeking Comfort, Not Freedom

This is the biggest mistake I see people making. The entire middle class is supposedly protected in this country. They live in this fantasy bubble of comfort. It's the 'I have enough' attitude.

Comfort is the enemy of abundance. The most dangerous element of finances is settling. It's the middle-class mentality. The entire middle class is built upon settling on comfort, on just enough. Just enough income, just enough to save, just enough invested—if you just get a house and a job that you like just enough that makes you just enough money. This mentality will never make you wealthy.

The wealthy seek freedom, not comfort. The wealthy seek so much abundance that it appears to others that they are greedy, but that says more about them that it does you. More is the mantra to wealth. Comfort isn't even on the menu. Make freedom your focus.

Life will discipline the comfortable until they either get off their ass and seek freedom or until they are very uncomfortable.

Top Money Mistakes

Diversification

I know you have been sold this idea of diversifying your investments. But it's a lie put on you from Wall Street because they need you to diversify. The truth is if you have 100 different investments you need someone else to manage them. That's why Wall Street has sold you on diversification. Diversification is the basis that all these big funds are built on and why Wall Street continues to get so rich.

My friend Mark Cuban said, "Diversification is for idiots." Andrew Carnegie said, "Take all your eggs and put them in one basket, and watch that basket!" The super rich go all-in on one or two bets and make them work. They don't have a thousand investments—not in the beginning. I don't want you to diversify in the beginning I want you to focus on growing wealth not conserving it – that is for later in life when you move into conservation rather than creation.

By the way, diversification of investments is different than the concepts of creating multiple flows of income so don't confuse them.

Figure out one space that you understand everything there is to know about and you know for sure without a doubt that it can't be destroyed, and protect that one investment. Find the thing you love and understand and go all in on it. The way to reduce your risk after all is control, responsibility and knowing what the hell you are doing!

Top Money Mistakes

Depending on One Income Flow

The holy grail of wealth is creating multiple flows of income. Imagine hundreds or thousands of income flows coming in every month or even every day. When I say income I'm not just talking about money coming in—I'm talking about opportunities, calls, ads, recruits, favors, likes, fans and on and on. Never depend on one flow of traffic no matter how big it is or you become dependent on one thing.

I know people who make 300K or 400K but it is all one income—they don't have investments and they are not wealthy, because they know that one thing could come to an end. When that income stops, they are going to be in trouble. It's rich for a moment, but to create real wealth you must make investments that will create dependable income streams or flows over long periods of time.

You want to be wealthy, not rich. You want wealth and income.

To start, figure out how you can make your one income flow a little bigger. Whether you make 3K or 10K a month it doesn't matter—make 3K into 4K and 10K into 12K. After you figure out how to make that first flow bigger, start thinking about getting a second income stream going. Ideas could be getting into a multi-level marketing company, a second job, mowing a lawn—something that will at least get a drip going. If you are a teacher, a waiter, a bus driver, a plumber, a cook—whatever it is you do, you need to get a second income flow.

Questions:
Personal Finance

1. What is personal finances defined as?

2. Why do most give up on their financial freedom?

3. Do all wealthy people use credit cards? Yes / No

4. When you have incremental growth or surges in income, what should you do with it?

5. What is indicated by you being concerned about the cost of something?

Questions: Personal Finance

6. Should you do business with someone you can't ask hard questions?

7. You must disregard your feelings when it comes to trusting others in business and demand _____.

8. What is the enemy of abundance?

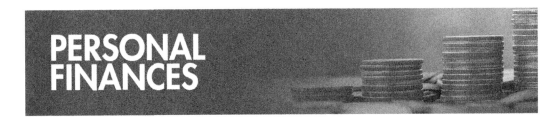

PERSONAL FINANCES

Personal Finances: Start With Your Mindset

I was not born into wealth.

I have worked very hard my whole adult life to create wealth a nd success for myself, my family, and my community. I do not ever blame someone or fault them for being poor. But I don't tol erate people who continue to stay in the mindset that bei ng poor is a permanent condition or something they cannot cha nge.

I teach people how to increase their income. I have heard the worst cases, people who were handicapped, people who were addicted to drugs, people with too much debt—I have heard it all and I promise you that there is nothing so bad that you can't overcome it and get rich—except a poor mindset. The reason ma ny people have no money is because they've been educated all wrong on the topic.

As we transition to the next course, I want to give you several ways you've been taught a wrong mindset. You have heard mos t of these since you were a child. Think about how much misi nformation you've taken in over the years.

Middle Class Money Lies & Limitations

A penny saved is a penny earned.
Fly under the radar.
Finances are complicated.
Buy a house and settle down.
A house is an investment.
Invest in a 401k.
Diversify your investments.
This is not the way to wealth.
Be patient.
Patience is a virtue.
Money doesn't grow on trees.
Money won't make you happy.
You can't take it with you.
Don't talk to strangers.
Save for a rainy day.
Not everyone can be rich.
You have to go to college.
Don't put all your eggs in one basket.
All debt is bad debt.
You can't get rich working for someone else.
Rich people are greedy.
I just need enough to be comfortable
More money equals more problems.
It takes money to make money.

Grant Cardone

Course 2
The Millionaire Mindset

Creating the right mindset is of vital importance—I can't stress this enough.

You are already rich and the fact that you don't know this is where the problem starts. You have 80,000,000,000 cells in your body, which makes you a billionaire many times over. You are probably having a birthday today, at least one of those cells are, and you aren't even celebrating.

Before you ever get financially rich you have to change your mind about money and life. You know you are operating below your potential so something is wrong! It's been said that what you think, you are. It's true. Do you truly believe you are a millionaire?

Everyone is a millionaire in something. How many times has your heart beat? How many breaths have you taken? You see, you already are a millionaire. There are many ways to be a millionaire. Are you a millionaire in not making things work, a millionaire in excuses, a millionaire in being late? Now the question is what do you want to be a millionaire in?

The Millionaire Recipe

- **2 parts Mental**
- **1 part Mechanical**

Whenever you cook something, you follow a specific recipe to get a specific result. The basic ingredients for your millionaire recipe are two parts mental and one part mechanical. Most people think the mental is the easy part—but they are wrong.

The mental parts are more difficult than the mechanical. Everything always goes back to mindset. You can lose the right mindset in an instant—someone says something, you lose confidence, and it all goes away. Becoming a millionaire takes mental fortitude. You have to reinforce your mind over and over again by what you read, listen to and those you spend your time with. The mental part is not just a one-time event.

As we dive deeper into the mental recipe keep in mind that you can't overlook this part. Your mentality is going to determine the success you create, have and determines whether you are able to enjoy it or not.

Takeaways:
1) Wealth is one part mechanical and two parts mental
2) Reinforce your mind over and over again
3) The mental part is going to determine the success you have and enjoy.

Millionaire Belief

You only need to believe in two things at this time;
1) The possibility of becoming a millionaire or super rich
2) Believe in me

Most people don't believe getting super rich is even possible. They think it's pie-in-the-sky, but you must believe in the possibility. Can you truly imagine yourself as a millionaire? Can you honestly picture your bank account having seven figures? If not, you can't move forward. Get your mind around the possibility that it can and will happen.

Secondly, you have to believe in me. I'm a hecta-millionaire, meaning I've become a millionaire 100 times over. I know how to create wealth, keep it and multiply it. You must believe I can take you there. If you don't believe in the source of your information the information you consume will fail you. Have you ever had a teacher you didn't believe in? You're aren't going to learn from someone if you don't have confidence in them. And don't try to get information from fifty different mentors or you will get confused. Pick someone and believe in them.

Believe in me, and believe in the possibility that you will be a millionaire. You don't even have to believe in yourself, just the possibility of this and me. These are the two mental things that you must get right for this recipe to work.

Why Most Don't Believe

In a poll of over 750 people, 45% gave their parents a grade of D for the education they provided in regards to money. What grade would you give your parents: A, B, C, or D? Half of what your parents taught you is holding you back. Your parents' job was to protect you. It was useful at one time and now it is a liability. You want to be successful—you don't need protection--you need to take risk.

Think about these things your parents taught you:

- **Don't talk about money**—It's no wonder that people don't have money if it's not something that can even be discussed. Meet weekly with your family to talk money matters.

- **Eat everything on your plate**—Why? Will you get rich by stuffing yourself? I always leave food on my plate. This saying comes from having a shortage mindset when you need an abundance mindset.

- **Get a good education**—This is why so many young people go into massive debt. They then find themselves still unable to get a high paying job. College will not teach you how to get rich.

- **Don't blow your own horn**—Muhammad Ali told the world he was the greatest even before he was. Likewise, I'm not afraid to tell the world I'm the greatest salesman in the world. Blow your own horn.

- **Set 'reasonable' expectations**—Stop settling and stop lowering targets. You want to dream big and have high expectations. Keep reaching higher and don't be "reasonable".

- **Don't talk to strangers**—The truth is strangers have everything you want. Who's got your money? Strangers. You must learn to talk to new people in order to expand and grow rich.

Takeaway: Your parents probably didn't believe in the possibility of getting rich, and they taught you their beliefs.

CREATING THE MILLIONAIRE MINDSET

Quit Making Excuses

You must not let your upbringing be an excuse for today. I got wrong messages as well growing up but didn't let that stop me. You are responsible for creating wealth and success in your life no matter your past. You are responsible for creating for your future. There are millions of excuses you can make but you alone have the steering wheel in your life now. Believe in the possibility.

Despite all your troubles, challenges, spotted past, the mistakes,—you are the only solution to all of that. People blame their kids, a divorce, the economy, the police, politicians, an accident, bad breaks, their age, or any other number of bad, unpredictable things that come in life for why they are where they are.

I know that there are difficulties with life, health, and finances. Ultimately the excuses, reasons or whatever you want to call them will not change your condition in life, only you can.

No matter your challenges, the solution is you. Why? Because you can manage you. You can't manage the guy stealing from you, the bad copy, the employee who didn't do their job, the love that betrayed you, or the friend that misled you.

After it happens to you from then on its just an excuse and excuses are not part of how you will create a life of success and prosperity.

On the next page I want you to write down every excuse you have ever used for your life. Write them down – all the injustices, broken promises made to you, the bad breaks, everything – write them down.

All Your Excuses

1. _____

2. _____

3. _____

4. _____

5. _____

6. _____

7. _____

8. _____

9. _____

10. _____

11. _____

12. _____

13. _____

14. _____

15. _____

CREATING THE MILLIONAIRE MINDSET

My Commitment to Success

I am committed, from this date on, to never use these excuses, justifications, or reasons for my future success.

_____

NAME/DATE

Your Life is a Miracle

Miracle is defined as a highly improbably or extraordinary event, development, or accomplishment that brings very welcome consequences. Another definition is an amazing product or achievement or an outstanding example of something.

Are you are miracle or not? It's up to you. Do you choose to be an amazing product or achievement or an outstanding example of something? It's simple. God does not need to intervene to create every miracle.

Most of my teenage years I was described as 'out of control' and 'troubled.' In high school, I had problems with authority figures, which accelerated to abusing drugs and more decline. I became bitter and resentful. Later, in my early twenties, I got beat up so bad I nearly lost my life. I still have the scars today. My drug problem progressed to the point where I had to put myself in a treatment facility. At 25 I was financially and emotionally broke, I lacked direction, and I was a problem to society and to my family.

Today I'm financially well off and never been happier. I know where I'm going and what I'm doing. How did I go from being a problem to society who couldn't go one day without drugs to one of the top five most influential CEO's in the world working with Fortune 500 companies?

The question should be asked—how did this miracle happen? I decided to quit waiting for miracles and instead make a miracle out of my life.

Takeaways:
1) A Miracle is an amazing product or achievement
2) Quit waiting for God's miracles
3) Make a miracle out of your life.

Life at 100%

To make a miracle, an amazing product or achievement or an outstanding example of something out of your life you must operate differently than most.

You will benefit if you show up early and stay late. When you hit the wall never quit and keep going all the way into you get through to the other side.

Miracles happen when you quit putting half of yourself into something and put yourself 100 percent in. Giving 100 percent brings success in such large proportions that it changes lives forever. Doing things part way never feels as good as going over the top does. Go over the top. See, it's better to crash going all the way than to play it safe and never feel anything.

Try this: for no apparent reason at all start clapping. Go ahead and clap. Give a 5-second applause.

How did it feel? Did you give 50 percent to that applause? Was it 75 percent? Was it 100 percent? I doubt it. This time, I want you to go all the way. Put your hands together and applaud hysterically for no reason except that you are alive. Clap for a moment and give it 100 percent.

Now how do you feel? Does your body feel different? Do you feel the energy? That's what 100 percent feels like. Now shoot for that everyday.

Takeaways:
1) Commit to going all in all the time
2) Notice the difference when you hit 100%

Pick the Size of Your Problems

I don't feel good when I'm not going 100 percent. It's a great way to live being at 100 percent but it will create problems for you.

Being at 100 percent has caused me lots of problems, lots of judgments from other people and I've gotten into difficulties. People don't feel comfortable, think I am a loose cannon and may not want to spend time with me.

So make a decision, would you rather have problems living at 100 percent or the problems you get while living at 25 percent or 50 percent? You aren't getting through this life without problems so pick the problems that are worth having.

I want you to mentally be in this millionaire thing 100%. You need to go all in. Remember, I told you that the mental part of the recipe is the most difficult part. I'm being real with you. Doing anything 100% is not easy. You need to get your mental game on tight if you are going to do this right.

When you start going 100% with the goal being a million dollars, you will get new problems. Some people in your life might have a problem with your pursuit. You will be criticized because some people aren't going to like you going at 100% toward a million dollars.

Takeaways:

1) I never feel good not going 100%
2) Going 100% will lead to new problems
3) You aren't getting through life without problems so pick the problems that are worth having.

Life at Less than 100%

- 76% of Americans are living paycheck to paycheck.

- 62% of Americans have less than $1,000 in their savings.

- 65% of those 65 and older have less than $25,000 in retirement.

- 21% of all Americans have no savings account at all.

- 43% of American households spend more money than they earn.

- The defined middle-class Americans reaching lowest levels since the Great Depression.

- The median income of middle-class of households in decline for 27 years.

- Median wealth for middle-class households dropped an astounding 28% between 2001 and 2013 (Pew Research).

- Middle-class take home pay before expenses has plummeted to 43% of gross pay compared to 1970 when the middle class take-home was 62%.

- There are still 900,000 fewer middle class jobs in America than there were when the last recession began.

- 51% of all American workers make less than $30,000 a year.

- 48% of all adults under the age of 30 believe "The American Dream" is dead.

For your friends who think Money Doesn't Matter

- US ranks 19th in the world when it comes to median wealth per adult.

- The level of entrepreneurship in USA is at an all-time low.

- For each of the past 6 years, more businesses have closed than opened.

- The 20 wealthiest people in US have more money than poorest 152m combined.

- Top 0.1% of all American families have as much wealth as the bottom 90%

- Person with no debt and ten dollars has greater net worth than 1 /4 Americans.

- The number of Americans living in high poverty doubled since 2000.

- 48% of all 25-year-old Americans still live at home with their parents.

- One out of five people live in poverty.

- 46 million Americans use food banks each year.

- 1.6 million American children slept in a homeless shelter last year.

- The United States ranks 36th out of the 41 "wealthy nations" in child poverty.

- 41% of all children in the United States raised by a single parent are living in poverty.

- 70% of all Americans believe that "debt is a necessity in their lives".

Stats for the naïve who think money doesn't matter

- 53% of all Americans don't have a minimum three-day supply of nonperishable food and water stored.

- According to John Williams of ShadowStats.com, the real unemployment rate in US really 22.9%.

- The percent of men working in America has gone from more than 80% in 1980 to 65%.

- The labor force participation rate for men has plunged to the lowest level ever recorded.

- The inventory to sales ratio has risen to the highest level since the last recession.

- Manufacturing index is falling.

- Orders for "core" durable goods are falling.

- Nearly half of Americans don't have $400

- The amount of stuff being shipped by truck, rail and air inside the United States has been falling every single month.

- Corporate debt in the U.S. has approximately doubled.

- While Japan continues to print money, Japan's 10-year treasury has gone from 8% to less than .1% over the last thirty years.

- Despite the Federal Reserve increasing interest rates 10-year treasury has continued to drop hitting new lows of 1.35% this week.

- Health insurance premiums have increased by a total of $4,865 since 2008.

- The average U.S. household has, at least, one credit card and approximately $15,950 in credit card debt.

Stats That Indicate Emergency

- The number of auto loans that exceed 72 months has hit at an all-time high.

- Home ownership is at the lowest levels in 37 years.

- 41 percent of all working age Americans either currently have medical bill problems or are paying off medical debt.

- The total amount of student loan debt in the US has risen to 1.2 trillion dollars— more than all credit card debt.

- There are approximately 40 million Americans paying off student loan debt.

- In just the last eight years the US added 8 trillion dollars.

- The U.S. national debt is an admitted $19 trillion.

- US has over 3.2 trillion dollars in unpaid obligations.

- The average savings for 35-44 year-olds is $14,226.

- The average savings for 55-64 year-olds is $45,447.

This is not business as usual and you will benefit from understanding the reality of the current economic situation. Giving anything less than 100% is not going to get you to Millionaire status.

Takeaway: If you are average, you'll just be another statistic.

The Middle Class Mindset

Earning less and having less than you deserve is a form of being broke. The reality is too many people are making sense of not having enough because they are somehow not starving or living in a third world country.

Most people are better at getting rid of money than getting money. Too many people earn too little and spend too much and have too little.

It is no wonder to me that people are having such a hard time. It's because of this "Middle Class" mindset.

Did you know that 34% of all people born into the middle class will fall into poverty as an adult, have no emergency funds, and no retirement?

The 'settle mentality' of the middle class will be the biggest obstacle to you becoming rich.

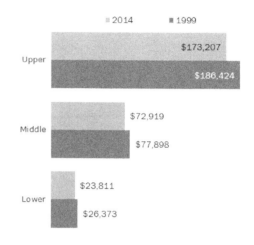

Median incomes of the middle class and other tiers fell from 1999 to 2014

Median income of households, by income tier, in 2013-14 dollars and scaled to reflect a three-person household

■ 2014   ■ 1999

Upper
$173,207
$186,424

Middle
$72,919
$77,898

Lower
$23,811
$26,373

Note: The income data collected in the 2000 decennial census were for calendar year 1999.

Source: Pew Research Center analysis of the 2000 decennial census and 2014 American Community Survey (IPUMS)

"America's Shrinking Middle Class: A Close Look at Changes Within Metropolitan Areas"

PEW RESEARCH CENTER

CREATING THE MILLIONAIRE MINDSET

The Middle Class Warning

The "middle class" is getting squeezed.

More people are getting rich and more people are becoming poor—the middle is getting hammered.

While the number of wealthy and the number of those who live in poverty both expand, the middle class gets smaller.

For the first time in 40 years, the share of American adults in middle-income households shrank from 61% in 1971 to 50% in 2015.

The "middle class" is falling behind. Your mommy and daddy's middle class is dying right before your eyes and will fail millions of those who are oblivious to it.

No politician can save what is already dead. Get out and get out quick.

The middle class is shrinking in most U.S. metropolitan areas, and lower- and upper-income tiers are gaining share

How the share of adults in lower-, middle- and upper-income tiers changed in 229 metropolitan areas from 2000 to 2014

160 metropolitan areas with an increase in share that are

Lower income

172 metropolitan areas with an increase in share that are

Upper income

203 metropolitan areas with a decrease in share that are

Middle income

Note: The shares of adults in the lower- and upper-income tiers may both increase in an area as the middle class share decreases, and this happened in 108 metropolitan areas. The 229 areas (out of a possible 381) are the ones identified in the source data and for which data are available for both 2000 and 2014. Middle-income Americans are adults whose size-adjusted household income is two-thirds to double the national median size-adjusted household income. Lower-income households earn less than two-thirds of the median, and upper-income households earn more than double. Incomes are adjusted for the cost of living in an area.

Source: Pew Research Center analysis of the 2000 decennial census and 2014 American Community Survey (IPUMS)

"America's Shrinking Middle Class: A Close Look at Changes Within Metropolitan Areas"

PEW RESEARCH CENTER

CREATING THE MILLIONAIRE MINDSET

The Middle Class Model

From 2000 to 2014 the share of adults living in middle-income households fell in 203 of the 229 metropolitan areas. The "middle class" isn't a set of rules based on earning—the "middle class" is a group of some two hundred million Americans who are being gravely affected by the new economy.

The reason people are in the middle class is not because of economics or politics or race or where you were raised, it's because of their thinking and actions. The concept of the middle class was sold to you. It was built on doing just enough, working just enough and saving just enough to say you are better off than most. You don't want to do just "enough" and have just "enough".

America has been sold the "middle class" model for generations. The freedom to make choices, the freedom to do what you want with your life and live where you want is not found in the "middle class" because the middle class is about comfort not freedom.

The middle class is an outdated dying model built upon the concept of work, save and rest. How much can you save when your income is going down? Why save when the banks don't pay you anything?

The "middle class" is diminishing quickly. Decide to become a millionaire—because millionaire is the new middle class

Takeaway:
1) The Middle Class Mindset of "just enough" is a dying model.
2) The middle class was sold to you.
3) The middle class is about comfort not freedom.

Today's Middle Class

1. Organics once and awhile

2. Two German Cars –Look at me!

3. Vacation with breakfast for two

4. Frequent flier miles

5. A job you don't like

6. Two weeks off

7. Two credit cards

8. 401K (who knows where that is)

9. Savings accounts .005% interest

10. Netflix account

11. A Home with a 30 year mortgage

12. College Debt

13. ATM Charges – You shouldn't have access to an ATM password.

14. Interest on Credit Card

15. Desserts – You've already over-eaten.

16. 32 oz. Steaks once and awhile

The Money Mistakes

When most people think about money mistakes they think about dumb stuff they spend money on or the investment they failed to make. But in reality that is not where most of us blow it.

The biggest mistake we all make is never making a decision to go for it in the first place.

In order for you to ever become a millionaire, I said that you first have to make the commitment and understand how important it is to become a millionaire. Millionaire is the new middle class. Then get your head right around this and surround yourself with people who are like-minded going after the same things. Here are the mechanical mistakes people are making:

1. Lacking millionaire math
2. Lacking Millionaire income targets
3. Not identifying who's got your money
4. Unable to continue to increase income
5. Not saving to invest

I'll go more into each of these, because the Millionaire recipe requires you not just to get your head right, but to do certain processes right as well. But before I can fix your mechanics, I must make sure you know how to properly make the mental decision to become a millionaire.

Millionaire Decision

To make a proper Millionaire Decision it takes more than just saying, "I'm going to be a millionaire!" Of course it starts with that, but there are actions which must follow.

If you wanted to be the world's best basketball player you'd have to do more than just say it. You'd have to remove all obstacles in your path that would prevent you from practicing more, reinforce your basketball decision every day to continue practicing like a maniac, economize all your activities to allow for you to practice hours on end, and add shooting, dribbling, and defensive skills to your arsenal.

Becoming a millionaire is no different.

1. Remove all obstacles & blocks
2. Reinforce & affirm decision daily
3. Economize all activities to this endeavor
4. Add income skills

I'll walk you through each of these because each of these are involved in your mental decision.

Takeaway: You must make a proper Millionaire Decision.

Make a list of obstacles & blocks you are aware of:

1. _____

2. _____

3. _____

4. _____

5. _____

6. _____

7. _____

8. _____

9. _____

10. _____

11. _____

12. _____

13. _____

14. _____

15. _____

CREATING THE MILLIONAIRE MINDSET

Obstacles and Blocks

How many times have you been told by someone that "cute" little saying that dismisses the importance of the things you want in your life, like getting rich and having success? I remember when I was starting to go hard at it and someone said to me, "Remember, Grant, success is a journey, not a destination." Please!

Success and getting rich isn't just a "journey" as countless people and books suggest it is; rather, it's a destination you should be in a damn hurry to achieve as fast as possible. And you and only you are in charge of it. So get rid of the knuckle heads that want to drop their little mental obstacles onto you.

No NFL club tells their fans the Super Bowl is a journey not a destination. Providing for your family, getting wealthy to bring freedom and choices to your family is more important than a Super Bowl so you have to decide who is on your team and who is just confused.

Friends and family need to be defined as either on your side, or not. There is no grey here. Just because I was born in the same house as you, sleep with you or went to the same school as you doesn't mean you're supporting me. And you are either supporting me or you are an obstacle to me.

If you aren't helping me get to where I am going then you are an obstacle to where I am going. It doesn't mean you are a bad person, it just means, if we are going to win the Super Bowl then I have to build a team of supporters.

Ruthless Clarity

Ruthless is a brutal word. If you look it up in the dictionary, it's got all negative connotations. It comes from the word ruth, a feeling of pity or distress or grief. Ruthless means without pity distress or grief. I'm telling you, be ruthless when it comes to friends and family. They will take you down if they're not on your side.

A lot of people don't know whose side they are on. You have people in your life, friends and family—who are against you becoming successful, not because they wish ill on you but because they have given up on their own dream and ambitions.

What do you do in that situation? The ultimate handling is to simply spend your time with those who want what you want rather than making time for people who have given up on what you want.

The second more difficult solution is to confront them and see if you can convert them. "Sis, get behind my dreams or you are going to get behind me." They'll say, "But I'm your sister —I helped raise you." "Yeah, you did a good job raising me, but you're not doing a good job supporting me now on where I want to go. You're either on my side or you're not—it's a black and white issue."

There are two groups here; one pulling for you and one pulling against. There are those that literally want you to do poorly—which is a very small group of people. That group doesn't even know that they've checked out of the game. The other group is HUGE and they want you to succeed.

You are either on my team or you aren't. The real question is whose team are you on? Do your friends and family know you made a commitment to success?

Black or White?

Make a list of people in your life - Either they are on your side or they are not.

Supportive	Non-Supportive
1. _____	_____
2. _____	_____
3. _____	_____
4. _____	_____
5. _____	_____
6. _____	_____
7. _____	_____
8. _____	_____
9. _____	_____
10. _____	_____

CREATING THE MILLIONAIRE MINDSET

Obstacles in your life.

The other obstacles in your life are not others but you. My friend Larry Winget once told me, "Before people make a list of all the things they want to accomplish they should make a list of things they are willing to give up."

When I first made a commitment to turning my life around I had to confront how many bad habits I had to break and how many things I had to learn.

What are you doing or not doing that is an obstacle in your own life. Make a list of all the behavior you are conscious of which could keep you from getting where you need to get.

Drinking	Cant see projects through
Smoking	Lack of Focus
Lazy	Anxiety
Depression	Cheating
Don't make cold calls	Don't follow up
Entitlement	Think your special
Hate Rejection	Introvert
Talk too much	Lack of confidence
Insecure	Lack of knowledge
Lack of discipline	Unable to get started

I have found it very valuable in my life to uncover flaws and deficiencies I wasn't even aware of.

Reinforce & Affirm Decision Daily

Once you surround yourselves with those who can support you and remove any obstacles and blocks from your path, you must reinforce and affirm your millionaire decision daily. This is why I created The 10X Planner. For 25 years I have created a practice of writing my goals down when I wake up and before I go to sleep. It's a simple task that builds tremendous fortitude and magic like fuel to your mission of financial freedom.

Getting rich requires huge commitment, action, discipline and persistence. And I believe creating wealth is an unselfish act.   Lets face it, you will have a hard time helping anyone else if you are still struggling to take care of yourself.

For my entire life, I have had this constant gnawing in me, knowing I can do more, achieve more, create more, give more, and help more. And I am most unhappy when I give up on that gnawing idea and most happy when I am pursuing it. Rather than being disillusioned by disappointments or deceived by small successes I continue to fuel my goals by affirming and reinforcing the successes I have yet to achieve, always with my attention on the future not the past. Whether they be failures or successes, they are the past.

I dare you to take the challenge of reaffirming your financial and success goals everyday twice a day for the next thirty days. Journaling with your attention on the future and creation is like like magic. Daily I pull out my 10X Planner and first thing I do in the morning is write my goals. Before I go to sleep at night I write them once again. Anytime I fail I pull out my 10X Planner and put my attention back onto the goals and future I desire to create.

Economize All Activities

Financial planners constantly stress saving or economizing money. What you must learn to economize is time and energy. When you start to create financial success the first thing to tighten down on is how you use time.

Be so busy that you don't know what day it is. Stacking your days is a must. Don't manage time, figure out how to create it by taking advantage of every moment. The more productive you are, the less distracted you'll be.

Create two columns on one sheet of paper. In column A, list the activities that won't ever contribute to your goal of being a millionaire. In column B list the distractions and activities you must do—the ones that will make you money. Now, avoid all activities in column A. It's that simple and seeing it on paper will increase your awareness of these potential and meaningless distractions.

Divide each hour into four 15-minute blocks of time and see how much you can complete in each 15-minute block. Work fast and furiously to see how much you can accomplish—make it a game. When you start to approach time this way, you start to move from one thing to the next with little room for disruption and wasting meaningless activities. The ultimate way to eliminate wasteful activities is to get completely obsessed with the ones that count. This method will cause everyday distractions to seemingly disappear.

The bottom line cut out all activities that no longer feed your ultimate goal. The wealthy understand what it means to say, "time is money." Economize it and then learn how to create it.

Economize All Activities

Contributing Activities	*Non Contributing Activities*
1. _____	_____
2. _____	_____
3. _____	_____
4. _____	_____
5. _____	_____
6. _____	_____
7. _____	_____
8. _____	_____
9. _____	_____
10. _____	_____

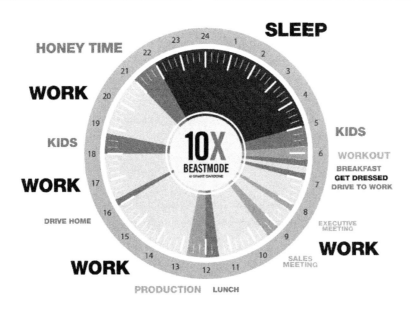

Add Income Creating Skills

If you've made the decision to get rich you will quickly realize you are limited on your income creating skills. It's not your fault. Knowing how to create new streams of income is almost non-existent.

When I realized I needed more income to reach my financial goals, I realized I didn't know how to increase my income. Sounds crazy but if you don't know how to increase income you won't increase income. I did not have the skills. I had to add sales skills to my abilities. If you want to get rich you need income-producing skills.

This is why I created Cardone University and have been adding content to this program for years so the employees in my company and other corporations and individuals I work with can learn effective ways to create income.

The best income skill you can add to your arsenal is to become an expert on how to find income and bring it under your control. There are many ways to produce income—a doctor, firefighter, pilot, teacher, police person, network marketer, write blogs, internet marketing, and etc., but to get rich you must learn how to ADD income and then add it again until you are able to multiply it into multiple streams of income. I am not talking simply sales here; I am talking about how to manage, create and then juggle multiple streams of new income over long periods of time.

But first things first – add the skill of adding income. We live on an economic planet and it only rewards those who are most committed to it. If you ever want to do more than just survive, you will have to add income skills to start making more money than you're making right now

Million Dollar Math

Now that we've gone over the mental areas, there are mechanical processes that you need to follow after your millionaire decision. The first thing to do is millionaire math. This isn't 2+2 but it's not calculus either. The goal of this exercise is to figure out all the ways you can make a million dollars. Doing this exercise will make things more real to you and give you motivation.

How many different ways are there to make a million dollars?
- $50K x 20 years
- $100K x 10 years
- $250K x 4 years
- $3000 a day

Do the math on what it takes to hit a million. If you make $50,000 a year and can figure out how to put away 40 percent of it (that is my saving target) it will take you 50 years times $20,000 per year to get there. If you don't do your math you won't get there because you won't have the right mindset. Math is a universal language.

Other ways:
- $100 product to 10,000 people
- $500 product to 2,000 people
- 1 gig $1,000,000
- 12 gigs $83,333 each

You get my point. How many different ways can you make $1m? The point is start doing some millionaire math. The bigger point is why haven't you already done the math?

Do Your Own Math

1. _____

2. _____

3. _____

4. _____

5. _____

6. _____

7. _____

8. _____

9. _____

10. _____

11. _____

12. _____

13. _____

14. _____

15. _____

CREATING THE MILLIONAIRE MINDSET

Retirement Math

Just for fun, let's do some more numbers. I did a recent survey where 94% of people thought they needed more than $500,000 to retire comfortably. More than five hundred thousand dollars. Maybe you don't think you will need that much. Well consider if you retire at seventy and live until you are ninety you will have to live on $20,000 a year or $1880 per month.

The truth is $1 million isn't even nearly enough—unless you want to live on $50,000 a year after taxes and Social Security? That's not counting inflation. And if $50K is your number forget about playing golf every day, traveling the world, not to mention some tragic illness not covered by your insurance.

Almost everyone is underestimating the amount of money needed to have a comfortable retirement. I'm not talking about savings accounts—which is basically mattress stuffing. Savings accounts will lose you money because interest rates don't keep up with the pace of inflation anymore.

The key to retiring is earning and investing. If you make 50K a year, it's going to be nearly impossible to save enough to retire. A penny here and a penny there will end up several pennies somewhere. The plan of buying a house, living in it for 25 years and paying it off to create wealth is a 1960's way of thinking—that nest egg plan is dead. You need to plan on living until you are 90 and plan on taking care of kids and grandchildren.

Do some big thinking math. Don't be afraid to calculate what you need to create $50 million dollars or $100 million or a billion.

Increase Income

Wages are not increasing. Real wages adjusted for inflation have been stagnant or in decline for almost thirty years in the USA. We are on the verge—if not already in— a new economic age. The old economy was a jobs economy, the new economy is the YOU economy. If it is to be its up to YOU not jobs.

Make a decision to focus on the "YOU economy" and take responsibility for your finances—starting with income, then adding income, then creating multiple streams of income then using surpluses of money to invest and increase income again.

Once you commit to millionaire status and do the math, the next step is to increase your income. This does not mean you take on a new job; it means you increase income. Your job is not just a place where you work; your job is to create financial freedom. Your job is where you get income and then can increase income again. You must think like an entrepreneur 24/7. Operate with urgency. Money doesn't care how old you are, the color of your skin, where you were born or went to school. Money ends up with those most committed to it.

Extrovert yourself and make your own economy by increasing income. Assume the economy is never going to get better and prepare for it to get worse.

Jobs are a part of the middle class and the middle class is disappearing. In 2008 I realized I was too dependent on THE Economy and not MY economy. I changed that and you can too. To increase your income you will either need to do more at your job to get more income, take on more jobs, increase skills so you can have a higher paying job, or learn how to sell, market, promote and increase your income.

Reasons You Are Not Creating Additional Income

Here are reasons why you haven't yet taken the time and effort to increase your income:

Entitlement—People feel they deserve money without earning it. You're owed nothing, deserve nothing, and are entitled to nothing just because you exist. Entitled people will never work hard enough to earn any real money because they feel things should be given to them. Nobody who accepts government handouts is rich—and they never will be unless they change their mindset. Slaves get just enough to survive—I'm not interested in surviving... I want to thrive! It feels good to have earned what I have.

Lack of Consistency—The rich make consistent routines in their life. A consistent approach starts with getting consistent in your day-to-day operations. When will you wake up? What do I do next? What do I do when I get to work? Get consistent and quit making it up. Successful people don't change their approach unless it doesn't work—they only change to change with conditions. I'm not perfect but I'm consistent. I go to bed at the same time each day, I eat the same foods, and I repeat the same actions over and over—I don't just wing it.

Reasons You Are Not Creating Additional Income

Normal Actions—Doing anything in life that society considers "normal" will only get you average at best. It's normal to work from 9 to 5—and it's normal to make $52K a year. This is why those who work just 9 to 5 will never be rich. They are taking average actions for their finances. The rich take massive action. Instead of 2 sales calls the average worker makes, the greats will make 20. Let's face it, even though there is plenty of money floating around on this planet, most people don't have much of it. It's because most people won't take more actions to get more money.

Unwilling to Use Debt—The Dave Ramsey's and Suzie Orman's will tell you to save and not take on any debt. The rich have debt. I have a lot of debt. If something can make you income, you should go into debt. My apartments make me money. I leverage debt to increase my net worth. Not all debt is created equal so you must learn to identify good debt versus bad debt and then start using good debt to your advantage. All the big companies—Google, Coca Cola, Apple—they all use debt. I was willing to go into debt and it paid off big for me.

Wrong Vehicle—The rich get in with the right company where there is opportunity for growth. My VP of sales Jarrod Glandt started working for me 6 years ago for $2500 a month. He wasn't making anything but he was in the right vehicle. He grew his skillset and has been able to multiply his monthly income many times over because he knew I was looking to expand. Too many people just look for a "job". You need a job, but you need the right vehicle. All companies live on revenue. Get commissions rather than just a salary and you will be in control of how much you earn. Look for ways to increase your pay at the company you are at.

Takeaway: There are several reasons why you haven't yet increased your income.

Magic Income Formula

Last year more than 500,000 households became millionaires just in America. Today, there are over ten million households that are "Millionaire" households in America, the highest since 2007.

Other people are doing it, and they aren't smarter than you. They just have figured out how to increase their incomes and what to do with their money.

You need an income target. Most people base their income needs on their salary, their immediate expenses and their debt. You must quit calculating your income needs based on your current situation and calculate based on where you want to go.

Use this magical Income formula to get ahead: Future Savings Monthly + Current Spending X 1.45 = income Target.

If I want to save $10K a month and already spend $5K, multiply $15K by 1.45 to get your target income of $21,750.   This allows for taxes and will net you the 15k you want. Can you go from where you are to $21,750 a month? Regardless of where you are and what you do I assure you, if you are committed, you can and you should!

Takeaway: Quit calculating your income needs based on your current situation or you will continue to be trapped in your current situation.

Magic Income Formula

Current Spending (monthly)   _____

Desired Savings (monthly)   _____

Total Income   _____

X 1.45   1.45%

Desired income Target   _____

if you get overwhelmed, break it down into how many ways you can do this

1) _____

2) _____

3) _____

4) _____

5) _____

My four year old daughter, Scarlett says, "It's impossible until you do it."

Who's Got My Money

Who's got my money is the secret question that will change your financial life. I have had a professional ball player tell me, "that single question changed everything for me."

That's the one question you must ask—and keep asking yourself. Unless you took over your daddy's business, you need money and should be spending your time each day serving those who have what you need. I hear some suggest you shouldn't monetize in the beginning. This sounds to me like the artist that is committed to starving.

Most of what you do in life you are never paid for. And when you are paid most the time you are underpaid. If you are ever lucky enough or persistent enough one day when you make it, you will be overpaid for almost everything you do.

Two major points to remember when it comes to money:

1) People want to exchange with you—If you bring great value people want to exchange money with you. Asking is not offensive to good people; they will want to pay you. I always have a product someone can buy from me because I take the time to create products that solve people's problems.

2) Your financial situation depends on new money. You need new money because you don't want to be dependent on any one thing to determine your income flow. No matter how big the one flow or one loyal customer, never never never depend on one flow for anything

3) Wanting to be paid fairly for what you give to the marketplace will only be looked upon negatively by those who are refusing to pay fairly.

Takeaway: Keep asking "Who's Got My Money?"

Strangers Have Everything You Want

The saying, "It takes money to make money," is simply not true. The saying instead should be "Strangers have everything you want." It takes contacts to make contracts, as a friend of mine once told me. Or how about "Your net worth is dependent upon your network."

Bottom line is you must network and make your contacts grow so you can grow your opportunities and grow your business. Remember your job is to create financial freedom.

Promote and market yourself 24/7, like you would if you were running for President. Your everyday routines are a way to capitalize and grow and extend your power base as I talk about in "Sell or Be Sold" and as I teach in detail in "If You're Not First You're Last."

I recently had a meeting with a bank to talk about refinancing some real estate. I shared my business card with everyone I came in contact with—from the guy who parked my car, to the receptionist, to the president of the bank. I even gave my card to the folks at the nearby sandwich shop. I said the same thing to each of them: "If I can ever do anything for you, please give me a call."

Make a commitment to being out there shaking hands, giving out business cards, making friends, kissing babies, and taking an interest in everyone you meet and then following up often and always. Then become omnipresent across all social networks until these same people you just met see you everywhere they go on the net. One more saying of mine, "If you don't know me you can't flow me."

Takeaway: Getting money from others means getting known.

Launching Into Orbit with Omnipresence

Today I will tweet over fifty times, deliver a live stream on Facebook Mentions that will reach over a million people, post a Facebook Q&A, deliver a periscope stream, respond to dozens of comments, write a blog, write at least one article, deliver 30 Snapchats, two interviews, and post at least one new video onto YouTube. I do this every single day, and sometimes I do much more.

You need to be fully committed. I also keep my eye on trending social media topics. For example, one day I saw #WhatBrokePeopleSay trending on Twitter, so I started banging out related Tweets like: "Will @GrantCardone loan me money?" It only took a few seconds of my time. Then, about every 15 minutes I posted new Tweets on the topic while making calls to people on my power base list—even ones I had already reached out to.

In a very short period of time, with no cost other than my creativity, I got attention for my brand. I engaged with followers, and added new followers to my power base. Try looking up trending topics for your market and think of creative ways to capitalize and launch yourself into orbit.

Money follows attention and your value in the marketplace is ultimately determined by how much attention you get, not how good your product is. Superior products that go unknown will not make as much money as inferior products that control the media. To orbit your finances first become omnipresent.

Takeaway: Attention follows money, the more attention you get the better your chances of getting money.

Stay Broke

I wrote about this before and this is a vital trick I have used to create monster surges in both income and wealth.

My first two big scores made over 5 million dollars because I used this practice of staying broke for eight years while I researched real estate and stashed cash away. When I started making more money I would immediately get rid of it, staying broke so I could one day be rich.

You must voluntarily put money away so that you won't spend it, use it, waste it or see it disappear. Don't spend what you make, but get rid of your new money and put it in a savings account until you have at least 100K stashed away before you consider investing any of it. This is a difficult thing to do and requires tremendous discipline on your part. Synonymous with restraint and self-control, discipline is a must to building financial wealth.

Most peoples' disciplines look more like bad habits instead of the massive, constructive actions that will provide them with wealth. Discipline is what you use to complete any activity until that activity results in success – regardless of how uncomfortable – and it eventually becomes your normal operating procedure. In order to attain and keep hold of success, you must determine which habits are constructive – and discipline yourself to do those things over and over again. Staying broke when you are making money is very difficult discipline and counter intuitive.

Takeaway: Stay broke until you get rich.

Save to Invest

The reason to save isn't to save—it's to have something to invest. I saved over a million dollars before I ever made my first investments. Why did I wait so long?

Because I waited until I knew exactly what I was doing and the deals were as close to sure things as possible. Warren Buffett says, "the way to reduce risk is to know what you are doing." My first two investments were slam dunks. I was in control, there was limited downside as I saw it and I was extremely certain of both investment projects rewarding me almost immediately.

If you don't want to be dependent on the government and government programs for your financial freedom, you must save to invest to create wealth. Most people simply save money for a rainy day or some future emergency and low and behold all the little money they saved gets blown on an emergency situation.

The only reason to save money is to invest it and one day become wealthy and financially free of all these programs that make people crippled victims and dependents. Save to invest; never save to simply save.

If you have less than a 100K, keep saving, until you bank a hundred. Why a hundred? Because it seems like enough money to demonstrate a real commitment to creating wealth. Then get to $250k and I will show you how to turn it into $5 million. I can't even advertise that, but I know I can do it. Its just that no one believes you can actually invest in things that turn out well because most people are investing in things no one even remotely understands.

Takeaway: Save to invest; don't save to save.

Why I Invest in Income-Producing Real Estate

I invest in real estate for several reasons.

Simple – Investing in real estate is a fairly simple activity compared to running more complex businesses.

Disruption Free – No technology can destroy the fact that people need a place to live, eat and sleep.   America is becoming a renter nation and it is my belief this trend will not be reversed.

Dependable Income Stream—One of the biggest benefits to income-producing Real Estate Investments is that the assets are generally secured by nine to fourteen month leases which provide a regular and dependable income stream that should produce positive cash flow.

Inflation Hedge—As countries continue to print money to spur economic growth income-producing real estate can act as hedge against inflation. Generally speaking, when inflation occurs, the price of income-producing real estate, should rise.

Physical Asset—Income-producing real estate is one of the few investment classes that has meaningful value as a hard asset. The property's land has value, as does the structure itself and the income it produces has value to future investors.

Leverage –Every dollar of cash should buy you 3X or 4X in real estate. The income will service the debt while paying down the mortgage.

Investing to Build Wealth

Your wealth depends on new money coming in that can be invested to create new streams of income. The first rule of building wealth is don't lose money. The second rule is remember Rule #1. If you don't lose money you will build wealth, especially if you continue to grow income and create new income flows. But that is not wealth; that is highly taxable income.

Remember this isn't about never being satisfied or greed it is about creating enough new flows so you can one day invest to create wealth. Wealth is almost not taxed at all. When I buy a building that is worth $25 million and its value improves over thirty years to $75 million, that increase in value is not taxed until it is sold.

Wealth typically gives you monster surges unlike income that comes much slower over longer periods of time. Again you save to invest to get your big wealth pops and surges in new income. Because not only did that investment go up in value but it also creates expanded income streams when invested in businesses that continue to grow income.

When investing
1) Know your investment.
2) No guessing.
3) No gambling.
4) If your aren't sure, don't do it.

Add Multiple Flows

The possible streams of income made simple:

Earned Income—Salary. Money earned for doing something. The money you are paid for your job whether it is working for someone else or even for yourself. The problem with earned income is it's taxable at the highest rate. But this is where everyone starts and until you are super wealthy, you will demand income.

In your lifetime you will mostly be underpaid and if you ever get truly great at something—then you will be overpaid. This is the first and most overlooked key to building multiple streams of income and creating wealth.

Profit Income—Money earned by selling something for more than it costs you to make or sell. For example, businesses selling their goods at a profit, whether at the retail or wholesale level, as distributors or manufacturers or as an affiliate. Profit is also taxed, but differently than income and that's why you want to be in business or have a side business if you can. Almost two-thirds of all businesses break even or lose money because they don't know how to sell enough to make a profit.

Interest Earned—Money earned as a result of putting your money in the bank or lending your money to someone else to use.

Dividend Income—Money that you are paid as a return on shares of a company you invest in. Dividend income is taxed at the lowest of rates. It's interesting, the more passive the income, the lower the taxes.

Multiple Flows

Rental Income—Money that you get as a result of renting out an asset that you have. This is where I have made most of my money and 90% of my net worth. Buying property requires money for down payments (typically 1/3rd of the purchase price) and then you better pay attention to that business. I started buying apartments when I was 35 and today I own 4500 units that have an average rent of $900 to $1100 per month. The game here is that the income exceeds all expenses, maintenance and debt allowing for a return on my cash invested.

Capital Gains—Money that you get as a result of increase in value of an asset, stock or company that you sell for a gain. When you buy shares at $10 and sell them at $21 - the $11 is capital gains, or if you buy a house for $200,000, spend $40,000 and sell it for $340,000, the $100,000 is your capital gain and you pay taxes at a much lower rate.

Royalties—Money you get as a result of letting someone else use your products, ideas, or processes. The Cardone Group in Orlando, Florida pays me a fee each month to use a sales technology I created for automobile dealers and that is considered a royalty. I am also a partner in the company and share in the profits of the company. A musician, writer, or inventor can be paid a royalty for something they created.

CREATING THE MILLIONAIRE MINDSET

Questions:
The Millionaire Mindset

1. Do you believe everyone is a millionaire in something?

2. The _____ parts are more difficult than the mechanical.

3. Are you just waiting for a miracle to happen or are you working to become one?

4. What was the median income of the middle class in 2014? Where is it now?

5. What percentage of those born in the middle class will fall into poverty as an adult?

Questions:
The Millionaire Mindset

6. The biggest money mistake we all make is never
   _____ in the first place.

7. What is the ultimate way to eliminate wasteful
   activities?

8. What is the best income skill you can add to your
   arsenal?

9. Millionaire Math: How much of your product or
   service will you have to sell to hit $1,000,000?

10. What are the seven possible streams of income
    made simple in this playbook?

How to Make Your Millions

Most millionaires won't have all of the income streams I mentioned - most of them will have simply taken a salary, saved it over long perio ds and one day realized they had become millionaires. But the really rich and wealthy will have multiple streams of income.

Billionaire Warren Buffet made most of his wealth using Capital Gains to earn most, if not all of his wealth—most of which is not taxable.

My friend Bob Duggan hit the Forbes 400 list by turning a company around. He never took a salary, invested his own money, convinced other people to do the same and then sold the company for $21 bill ion creating an enormous capital event in his life that was taxable because a sale was made.

I have created my wealth running companies and holding them priva tely so that I can operate them the way I choose. Two of the compa nies are thirty years old and while the products have evolved, t he purpose has been the same. One involves a partner. The real esta te company is completely different business and created a lot of wealth for me but I wouldn't have my real estate portfolio if not for t he income provided from the first two streams.

The point is there are many ways to create wealth and you have to find yours. As long as you are committed, add the necessary skills, surround yourself with like-minded people and never quit you will get there.

How to Make Your Millions

1. Make the Millionaire Decision

2. Do Millionaire Math

3. Set Millionaire Income Targets

4. Identify Who Has YOUR Money & Go Get It

5. Increase Income & Stay Broke

6. Save to Invest, Don't Save to Save

7. Create Multiple Streams

8. Repeat 1-7

Course 3

At 25 years old, I owed the government money but I always wanted to be rich. My entire life, I've always dreamed, "dude, what if I had a lot of money?" My neighbor, Lash Stevens, was the son of a doctor, and man, I'd watch this kid. He'd go boat riding. He'd go snow skiing. I'm like, snow, I didn't know there was snow. I'm a middle-class American in the South. They're going hunting! I'm like, hunting? I didn't have a dad to take me, my uncle was buried in his own work, he's got his five kids, and I'm sitting there thinking everybody else has got something going on but me.

But I changed my condition, and you can too. You don't have to be envious, you can get to a place where others are inspired by you. – Grant

You Don't Start a Business

You heard me correctly. You DON'T start a business. You ARE a business. If you go online and Google how many businesses are in America, it's going to say 28 million. The reality is there's over seven billion small businesses on planet Earth. My daughter, Scarlett, is an enterprise right now. She doesn't need to go get an LLC, she doesn't need to say she's the sole proprietor, she doesn't need to hire a lawyer, she doesn't need to get Ernst & Young to be her accountant, she is a business; she is a money-making, idea-generating, little creation machine.

That's if she chooses to be.

If the parents would just tell children to produce, they could actually build value, bring value, because they are each a unique proposition. All kids are, by the way, and you should be using them as assets in your business. Look at Donald Trump, look at Donald go. He might be a President of the United States of America. He is a business.

Business, what is a business anyway? Have you ever looked it up? Have you ever defined it? Have you ever taken a moment just to say what is a business? If you look it up in the dictionary, you're going to see it says, "the practice of making one's living by engaging in commerce". My billionaire friend Bob Duggan looks up everything, every word, in a dictionary. The guy sold a company for $21 billion dollars, so do you think you should start looking up words?

Takeaway: Don't think about "business" in the traditional, limited way.

The True Meaning of Business

I have an accounting degree, I went to college, and never looked up the word business. Again, the definition is the practice of making one's living by engaging in commerce. Well, I have to look up commerce. But before I looked up commerce, I looked up where the word business came from. Business comes from a word that means "a state of being busy.

What's that mean?

The state of being busy. How many of you have heard people say, "Man, you can't just do busy work." I'm telling you if you don't do busy work, you'll never do any business. You don't do any busy work, you're not going to do any business, period, you understand? Never! You have to do busy just to get into business. The original word, the derivation of the word business, comes from busy.

Busy, get busy!

Takeaway: If you aren't busy you aren't doing business.

Business 80/20

I'm going tell you right now, I didn't trust my good looks, I didn't trust my intelligence; I simply outworked everybody. I'm busy even when I don't know what I'm doing; I'm going to stay busy, I'm going to push, I'm going to shove, and I'm doing things I never get paid for. 80% of what I do, I never get paid for, I never expect to get paid for, until maybe later. 80% of what I do is busy work, 20% of the time, I expect to get paid.

Takeaway: Get busy and don't expect to always be paid for it right away.

Commerce

Get used to staying busy. Get used to showing up, stay busy, run fast, move as fast as you can from project to project. Commerce, let's look up commerce because the definition of business includes this thing called commerce.

Commerce: *"The activity of buying and selling"*

Clearly, a lot of people don't know something about business because they're buying stuff, but they never sell anything. "The activity of buying and selling", this is the simplicity of commerce, the simplicity of a business or a company.

Takeaway: Most college graduates don't know the definition of business or commerce.

Introverts in Business

The only reason I went to business school was to learn how to make money, and I got out of there with a five-year degree, owing the government money, and I didn't even know what the word commerce meant. Commerce means "the activity of buying and selling, especially on a large scale". This is critical and vital for you to know, because 28 million small businesses in America have no employees. By definition, that would not be commerce, because commerce is the activity of buying and selling, especially on a large scale.

I'm going tell you why businesses are failing today, why salespeople fail, why departments fail, why divisions fail, why companies and entire brands fail. Commerce also means, "the social dealings between people". That's just a little warning to you introverts out there. They make an excuse, "I'm an introvert I don't like talking to people!"

Do you like being broke?

Do you like just getting by?

What if I told you I was an introvert? I still am when I need to be. Listen, if you are an introvert get over it to get business done—stop using it as an excuse.

Takeaway: Commerce includes social dealings with people, so if you are an introvert get over it or your business will fail.

Two Classes

Most businesses don't work, they fail. It's not a political planet, it's an economic planet. The reason politicians don't tell you this, is if they announced this fact, the civilians would go crazy. The people, civilians, that word comes from being civil.

Nobody tells you go get rich. Why don't you go make $300 grand a year? Why not make a million dollars a year? There's two classes in America, the wealthy and everybody else. There's not three classes. There are two classes.

You are either rich or you're poor.

Takeaway: You are in one of two classes.

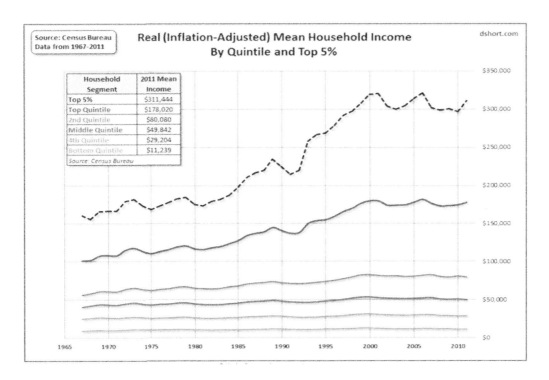

Look at this graph. Where do you want to be on it?

Takeaway: Get rich or be poor.

Income of Top 10 Countries + Tax Rate + Net Savings + Hour Worked

Country	Median Wage	Tax Rate	Net Savings Rate	Hours Work Per Week
USA -	$ 54,000	23%	4.0%	37.5
Ireland -	$ 51,000	19%	5.2%	31
Luxembourg	$ 53,000	28%	10.0%	32
Switzerland	$ 50,000	30%	13.4%	32
Australia	$ 45,000	23%	9.3%	35
UK	$ 45,000	25%	8.5%	42
Canada	$ 42,000	23%	5.1%	32
Norway	$ 44,000	30%	9.2%	30
S.Korea	$ 35,400	12%	5.3%	45
Netherlands	$ 29,000	38%	6.2%	35

created by GrantCardone.com

This is literally crazy. How can you live on $50K a year? How can you even live on $100K a year? Truth be told, I don't see how people live on $250K a year. It doesn't matter where you live, if you don't start making big boy money you will struggle with falling into poverty.

Takeaway: Regardless of your country, the financial realities are the same.

Savings in Depression

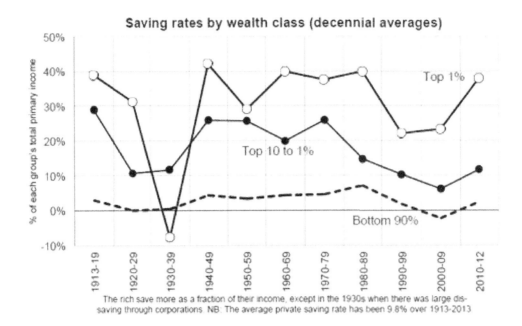

Saving rates by wealth class (decennial averages)

The rich save more as a fraction of their income, except in the 1930s when there was large dis-saving through corporations. NB: The average private saving rate has been 9.8% over 1913-2013

Source: Emmanuel Saez and Gabriel Zucman. The Distribution of U.S. Wealth. Capital

This graph goes back to 1913. This is before World War I, and there are three groups in this graph. This is showing savings. There's a top 1%, a top 10%, and then there's everybody else, the bottom 90%.

Now, there's only one time when that top 10% dropped, it was in the Great Depression.

Takeaway: Make millions now because another Depression can come.

"The worst kind of violence is poverty."

– Gandhi

HOW TO MAKE MILLIONS IN BUSINESS

Savings

The savings rates between 2000 and 2009 were the lowest in the last 100 years. We're at record low levels right now. Right after 2007, it spiked. It went from 3% to almost 12% because people got terrified. Why am I trying to scare you right now? I'm trying to get you back into scavenger mode, into hunting mode, into kill mode. Eat what you kill Don't hate those one percenters. Learn how to become like the 1%.

You know, I don't do fancy things. I have a plane. The only reason I have that plane is so I can get places as fast as possible. There's a reason I bought that plane, because I want meet people, be social, and do commerce by definition. The plane, by the way, was supported by the definition, 'large scale, meet people, conducting business'.

Takeaway: Get in save mode, live like the 1% and start conducting COMMERCE.

Problem Solving

If you are going to make millions in business you will have to solve a problem. What is the problem you're going to solve? Identify that problem. Solve a problem a lot of other people have so it's scalable. That could be a possibility. Oh, by the way, Uber, Velcro, Google, anywhere you solve problems, you'll find money. Problems equal money. The bigger the problem, the bigger the money. The bigger the global problem, the bigger the opportunity. Take TV on-demand. We created our GrantCardoneTV studio because of problems. My twin brother created a business out of nothing, a couple of years ago. He had a business that had merchant returns. He gets a phone call from Visa and says, "Sorry, your account's frozen." "Why is my account frozen?" "Your account's been frozen because you have a bunch of charge backs."

So he and his wife looked at the charge back industry, and figured out a way to reduce people's charge backs. His company did $16 million in gross sales last year. He's going to net about 44% of that. The business is still young. That's the problem he solved. What can you do? My brother understands business. He understands commerce. He's willing to be social. He's willing to go large. What is the problem he can solve? He can solve a problem for other merchants. Oh, who's his audience? His audience is going to be business to business, business to consumer, hybrid, retail, direct sales, inside sales, e-commerce.

Who's your audience? So, that's a question you have to ask and then do the math. The math I did was this. Can I sell a $400 product? I asked myself that question. I just asked, what number can I sell to the public? Is there a number that I can sell to the public? I said, "Yeah, I think, I could sell a $400 product."

Problem Solving

I was about 30 years old, wanted to start a company. I had some experience calling on businesses. I knew sales. I knew how to talk to people. I had spent four or five years educating myself on sales. I can do that. Maybe you're a housewife. Maybe you love kids. Maybe you're a nanny. You're like, "Hey, man, what can I do?" I'm a nanny, man. Is that a problem? Yes, it is. My wife and I don't want to be with our kids 24 hours a day, seven days a week. Would the Cardone's pay anything for that? Probably would, right? So, I'm like, OK, I could sell a $400 ticket, so I start doing math. This is where you start your company. I need to sell 25,000 people a $400 product.

I would need to sell a $400 product to 210 people a month. There's your math. Can I make 50 sales a week? Where's my audience? Who do I talk to? How do I get in front of them? That makes a million dollars. I'm just trying to simplify it for you. Now, why do you want to make a million dollars? Cause the middle class is crushed. It's not coming back. Nobody's going to bring it back. If it could have come back, it would have come back 10 years ago. It's not coming back. It's going to get worse, not better. This country is $20 trillion in admitted debt. I think they say it's $19 trillion. Who cares? They said that Iraq would cost $1 billion. It cost $3 trillion. That's all we know. All we know is the powers that be lie. Every group lies. The Democrats, the Republicans, both sides.

Takeaway: Simplify things. Pick a problem, do some math.

Build an Offer

Years ago this guy Jarrod Glandt found out about me. Jarrod says, "I could go start my own deal, or, there's this guy, Grant Cardone and he's got a company. I like what he's doing. I like the way he talks to people. I like the way he's willing to use technology. I could go solve some problems for Grant." Jarrod has been working for me for years and now he's my VP of sales and a millionaire.

You don't need to go start your own company. Find somebody that's rolling, man, somebody that's expanding, somebody that's got a vehicle with fuel in it and wants to accelerate, that wants to embrace technology.

Takeaway: You don't have to start a business, you are a business that can work for someone else.

You—A Business

So Robert, my video guy, comes to me and says, "Hey, what else can I do here?" I say, "Let's sell some other products here. Let's sell some video production. Let's produce video for people. Let's produce video that's so sick that other companies want to call us. Why don't we produce some advertising, some commercials?"

Now Robert has three streams of income instead of just one and he's more than doubled his earnings from the previous year.

If you want to pay attention to the money, look, you have to go look for a million dollars to find it. You aren't going to find the Easter eggs without hunting for them, right? You have to believe in something. Otherwise, you get leftovers.

Takeaway: Brainstorm what you can do at your job to earn more money.

You—A Business

The United States constantly prints money. Everybody should have more money. I got fired once. I worked at McDonald's. I quit McDonald's because I smelled like french fries every night. I hated it. My boss said I had a bad attitude.

My boss didn't hate his job because he ran the place. He ended up running six of them. Ended up owning four of them. The mindset is different.

One guy's just participating, sitting on the bleachers, the other guy's saying, "Hey, I'm playing on the field."

Show me a rich guy or gal, and I'll show you somebody who did something that everybody else thought couldn't be done. And then, when they did it, everybody else said, "Man, why didn't I do that? I could've done that. I had had an idea like that, right?" But you didn't do it. I could have done an excellent job at McDonalds and worked my way up, learned the business and owned lots of franchises. But my heart wasn't in it when I worked there. I didn't see myself as a business, I just wanted my five bucks an hour.

Takeaway: Your job can have opportunity if you see yourself as a business.

Pitch Building

Again, what can you do? Why is that important? Hey, I want to go to Mars. I want to fly, personally fly, with just a body, to Mars. I can't do that. There's no reason to try to build a business around that. First thing is, what can you do? Second thing is, what problem can you solve on this planet, right here, right now. Not in the future.

Who is your audience? Who's the audience you can sell to? Who's the audience that you can approach? Who do you already know in the marketplace that needs your product, that wants your product? You want to sell a million dollar product. Who's your audience? It's probably not the people that live in your neighborhood. It would have to be people that have a million dollars, and have the problem you can solve. What's the offer? What's the commercial? You've got to build a commercial out. A 20-second commercial. Build a pitch.

Takeaway: Having an idea to solve a problem is not enough, you must build a pitch.

The Perfect Pitch

A pitch is like a commercial. It shouldn't be more than 20 seconds. If you can't tell your story in 20 seconds, you have a problem.

One of my pitches is "My company increases sales by 15 to 20 percent, and we'll do that in less than 14 days. Who in your company would make that decision, if what I'm saying is true? That takes 16 seconds.

You've got to have your pitch down to a commercial that you could drop on the radio or TV that would tell your story. And then you've got to go sell it. This is where your business fails. Nobody wants to do the ugly job.

I'm building up my real estate portfolio. I've got millions of dollars worth of real estate, and we're going to take that to four billion, and I hired an analyst to come in here, and I told him, "Look, this is a sales game." He replied, "Oh, I'm not a salesman." So I told him, "Then you can't be an analyst."

If you're not a salesman, you can't be an analyst. Because we aren't going to have anything to analyze. We have to find a buyer for our product, or I have to find a seller so I can acquire property, or I need to find a buyer so I can dispose of property.

Takeaway: Pitching is vital, and you have to know how to sell to pitch properly.

Pitching

Are you ready to perfect your pitch?

Clarify your goal. What is the objective and goal of your pitch? What is the one thing you want this person to do when the pitch is over? Do you want to tell potential clients about your organization and make them a client? In my case, I want the person across from me to know what I do, see how he or she can benefit, and decide within 20 seconds that I am the best person with whom to do business.

Takeaway: Whatever you are selling, you must first clarify your goal when you start making your pitch.

Pitching

Ask for attention. If you don't get attention, you'll just be talking. The best elevator pitch demands that you get the person's full attention. All you have to do is ask for it. "Can you give me your attention for the next 20 floors to share with you what I do?" Ask for attention before you start your pitch.

Takeaway: We live in a noisy world, a good pitch must get a person's attention.

"Find your WHY or you'll never find your HOW."

– Grant Cardone

HOW TO MAKE MILLIONS IN BUSINESS

Pitching

Make it sticky. When you move into your pitch, make sure that the first thing your audience hears is sticky (keeps their attention.) The easiest way to do this is to make a giant claim where your unique value proposition is clearly stated. Start your pitch by describing what your organization does and do it in one sentence that sticks. Here's an example: "We help businesses increase sales by 15 percent through identifying missed opportunities." That is sticky, pointed and memorable.

Having trouble coming up with a sticky point? Ask yourself: "What is the one thing I want this person to remember when this pitch ends?" Your claim should generate interest or suggest who in the company would be best to contact. Your elevator pitch must hit very hard and be sharp and pointed so your audience remembers it.

Takeaway: Make big claims so it's memorable.

Pitching

Determine the decision maker. In any pitch, you want to know who the decision maker is. This is especially true with the perfect elevator pitch. There is no reason to pitch any further without knowing who can make a decision. Immediately following the big claim, ask, "Are you the person that could make a decision to invest $40,000 to increase sales by 15 percent?"

Takeaway: In order to make any sale you have to talk to the actual decision maker.

Million Dollar / Year

$ 83,332   per month

$ 19,203   per week

$ 2,778   per day

$ 278   per hour

What can you do to hit these marks? What can you sell, at what price, to how many people? Get a pitch and make it happen.

START A MILLION DOLLAR BUSINESS

but remember…

YOU ARE A BUSINESS ALREADY

Small Business

91% of small businesses in America make less than $250,000. That's 91% of 28,000,000 small businesses. You just need to know the truth. The truth is that median income America's not doing well. Minimum wage is not the issue, the people that are doing well are in the top 10% of the owners on this planet, period. I can go back and show you stats. Every stat indicates the same thing.

76% of all small businesses in America break even or lose money. What does break even mean to you? Why would you start something to break even? Bloomberg says 80% of all entrepreneurs are failing within the first 18 months. No cash flow, no reinvestment. Without cash flow, they can't hire people. The number one question I get asked here every day is this, where do I find good people? No cash flow means you cannot hire good people. If my company made $250 grand a year, we'd have three people here. I wouldn't even be doing this.

Takeaway: Don't be a small business, you must get big. Think growth.

Making a Difference

Making a difference in the lives of others is worth all the money you could ever stack up. It's not the money that puts a smile on your face, it's the memories of what you did to help. From time to time you'll hear back from these people that "you made that difference." Because if you don't make the difference, you're not going to have the money. The money doesn't allow you to make the difference. You make the decision, I'm going to make a difference, I count, I'm here.

Takeaway: To make a difference you have to get big, grow giant. Stay small and you'll make no impact.

Don't Stay Small

54 percent of small businesses in America make less than $25,000 dollars, that's $2,000 dollars a month. $2,000 a month?! I'll pay you more than that from the get go, if you're talented. Small doesn't work and what I want to convince you to do is to get out of the myth of small, as if it's more manageable. This is what people think, "I'm going to do small because it's more manageable to be small"— it's not. It's less manageable. I'm going to provide better quality- this is a mistake I made in my first company. I made the mistake of thinking I'm going to offer better quality because I'm small. I thought I'd have a handful of clients. That is a disastrous error for your to make; you cannot have a small number of quality customers. It's impossible. Get out of this small thinking.

Takeaway: Small does not equate to quality.

Staying Small

How can you hire someone and spend $25 grand if you have $6000 in the bank?
You can't. You can raise it or borrow it, but you've got to have confidence and
guts and you've got to know what you're doing. It goes back to what Buffett says
—In the risks you take, you reduce your risk with knowledge. You're going to get
better quality if we produce 500 videos here, we're going to produce better
quality than if we produce five. 500 movies will produce better quality then five
movies. 5000 movies would produce a better quality movie than five movies,
why? Because I get quantity; quantity becomes magic. Don't believe that you'll
go to work for yourself, do everything yourself, have no employees. The only
thing big about that is your lack of commitment. Small sucks.

Takeaway: It takes knowledge and confidence to grow.

Small Sucks

It is easier to manage and less risk now having 45 employees than when I had 5. Now is it more problems? Yeah. I've got 40 more problems I didn't have then. But we got more income too, to solve some of those problems. I think I can live with that problem. People do not cost money; employees do not cost money. Employees should not be seen as an expense. The last thing, the last myth of the business is that you scavenge, you think you're going to scavenge. What that means is, I'm going to be the small company and I'm going to go nip at Coca-Cola or Google or the big Facebook, I'm going to go nip at them. No, you're not. You're going to get run over by them.

Takeaway: Staying small will get you run over.

Who is your audience?

- B2B
- B2C
- Hybrid
- Retail
- Direct sales
- Inside Sales
- E-Commerce

Whatever your product or service, you must define your audience in order to perfect your pitch.

Go sell it

- Know your customer
- Know why people buy
- Build a pipeline
- Justify value

1 Million Isn't That Big

There has been a lot of discussion recently about raising the minimum wage. Minimum wage is not the problem in this country; median wage is the problem.. The truth is a million dollars today is not big money; it is the new middle class.

Aim for multi-millions and adjust your mindset that a million dollars is the new average.

Takeaway: Quit following your daddy's dream and make your own. Go for $50 million or more.

"SMALL BUSINESSES NEVER SURVIVE."

– Grant Cardone

HOW TO MAKE MILLIONS IN BUSINESS

You Aren't a SMALL Business

I'm a business. You are a business. You've got a W-2 form. Your name is Joe, you make $52,000, that's your company. My friend Bob Duggan fixed his financial situation, he took his finances and said, "Hey, I'm going to go get this money."

Takeaway: You are on a hunt; getting a million dollars is in no way a passive activity.

You Aren't a SMALL Business

Have the confidence to re-invest in new programs and new promotion for your business. Flat lines always fall. If your income is flat, picture it as a heart beat—you'd be dead. Hospitals would be sending you to intensive care. Numbers don't lie. Start a business, or build value in the business you're in. Become so valuable to your company that people throw money at you so that you can actually take care of your household.

Takeaway: Getting big will require your investment. Don't flat line.

Facts About Businesses

76% of all small businesses break-even or lose money.

Takeaway: I've told you this statistic more than once because you need to know that staying small will not make you millions.

Facts About Businesses

Bloomberg Business Statistic:

80% of entrepreneurs are failing in the first **18 months**.

Takeaway: You don't have to start a business, you ARE a business.

$250,000 Small Business

Income	250,000
Minus Expenses(60%)	150,000
Equals Adjusted Gross	100,000
Minus Taxes (40%)	40,000
Leaves Profit	60,000
Less Salary	60,000
Equals Cash Flow	NONE

Takeaway: Small business will not give you the cash you need.

No Cash Flow Means...

- Can't hire
- Can't keep staff
- Can't promote
- Can't invest
- Can't sleep

Takeaway: Go big or go home.

Business Failures Made Simple

Businesses and people fail when they don't sell products and services in quantities great enough at prices high enough to provide a cash flow significant enough to grow.

Takeaway: This is why small businesses fail, they lack quantity.

Scaling

If you want to save money, as a way to get where you want to get, this is how you save money. If you're 20 years old and you save $360 a month, you'll eventually get there but it will take a long time. You say I'm going to go to the marketplace and I'm going to start a company or I'm going to be a company within a company. Simplify your business. I can start a business right here, right now. I'm going to go sell cups. Grant Cardone cups, I'm going to grab a cup somebody else built. I'm not going to manufacture it, I'm going to put my label on the outside. I'm going to go to the marketplace. I bought the cup for $3, I'm going to sell it for $15, I've got a five X mark-up. Now I have to push it into the marketplace. I'm going to take the money left over from that sale of $10. $10 isn't much money, so I have to do it a bunch of times, I have to scale it out.

Do I solve a problem with the cup?

I don't know. Do I solve a problem? Does it improve conditions? Does it make things better for someone? If it doesn't, you don't have a business and it's not scalable. If your product doesn't solve a problem for someone, they won't pay for it.

Takeaway: Scaling requires problem solving.

Love Doesn't Make a Business

Everybody's got ideas. Just because you love something doesn't mean it's a business. I've seen this on Shark Tank at least 12 times. "I love it, I love it, it's a great idea. I just know, I just know it's going to work because I love it." Just because you love it doesn't mean it's going to be a business.

Takeaway: Never assume a passion or love can be a business.

"MILLIONAIRE IS THE NEW MIDDLE CLASS."

– Grant Cardone

Fast is the New Big

Fast is the new big. I had a guy tell me the other day, "Be patient, Grant." The patience thing is for somebody else, it's not for me. I don't want to do the patience thing, I want to do now. Be the hare to be the multi-millionaire. Today you must be steady and fast and you need to be steady and there every day.

Takeaway: There's nothing good about being a tortoise without also being the hare.

THE "SAVE YOUR WAY THERE" MYTH

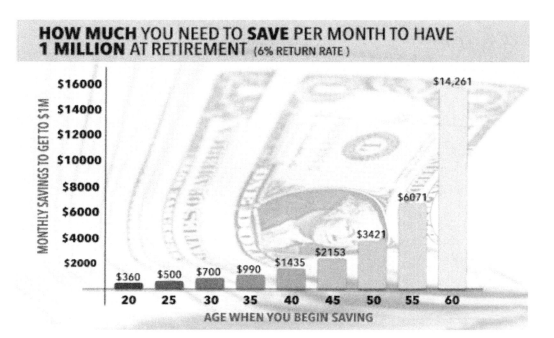

HOW MUCH YOU NEED TO **SAVE** PER MONTH TO HAVE **1 MILLION** AT RETIREMENT (6% RETURN RATE)

MONTHLY SAVINGS TO GET TO $1M

$16000
$14000
$12000
$10000
$8000
$6000
$4000
$2000

$360 $500 $700 $990 $1435 $2153 $3421 $6071 $14,261

20 25 30 35 40 45 50 55 60

AGE WHEN YOU BEGIN SAVING

HOW TO MAKE MILLIONS IN BUSINESS

Types of Businesses

- Sole proprietorship
- Partnership
- Limited Partnership
- Corporation
- Limited Liability Corporation
- Non-Profit

Takeaway: Don't get caught up in what to do, just start and figure it out later.

"Be the Tortoise _and_ the Hare."
– Grant Cardone

Simplify your Business

1. Solves a problem

2. Improves conditions

3. Provides positive cash flow

4. Scalable

Takeaway: Use this simple checklist before starting anything.

"Love me or hate me, at least you know me."

– Grant Cardone

My Biggest Mistakes in Business

Small think... I thought too small from the age of 29, until the age of about 42. It wasn't until I met my wife that I started thinking big. Whether you're excited about your brand new startup or you're starting to lose excitement from objections, conflict, lost revenue or a bad business plan—none of that matters. The reality is you can't grow your startup to a grownup business without operating with urgency, utilizing your haters, staying focused and growing your business.

Takeaway: Think big from the beginning.

Business Mistakes

I underestimated the potential of the marketplace, the potential will last longer and is bigger than you can ever imagine. I remember when I started my seminar business at 30 years old, I was out marketing, This seminar promotion company came along, they were behind me for a year. We had done a tour of all the cities in America and did 50 gigs in one year and I asked the owner, "Bob, how many of these can we do? He's like, "Grant, what do you mean?" I said, "We've been doing this for a year, how long can this last?" He's like, "You're going to be doing this, you're so good, you're going to be doing this when you're 50, 60 years old if you want to." And I thought it didn't have the longevity. I continued to revamp, re-invent myself. The market is so much bigger now than I imagined back then.

Takeaway: Your market can be huge but it might take a revamp or reinvent on your part to make it work.

Business Warnings

I didn't re-invest money fast enough, I was scared in the beginning. If I made $30 grand, what I did was I'd take that $30 grand and I put it away and I wouldn't touch it. I should have been re-investing part of that money, I should have split a little bit, put a little off to the side and not spent it, and I should have taken that other money and re-invested it back in the company. That was a big mistake.

Takeaway: Reinvest back into your business early.

Business Warnings

Somewhere between 2001 and 2009, I started getting fat and sappy, and I started resting on my laurels, thinking I was the winner, comparing myself to other people. You will always pay a price for resting on your laurels. Stay on the hunt, stay hungry, keep pushing.

Takeaway: Don't assume you've "made it."

Business Warnings

I trusted without proof. I made a monster mistake at the age of 40. Some guys came to me. They loved me; they found out what was important to me, they joined that venture, and they said, "Hey, let's do some business together." I didn't say, "Hey, show me your freaking income statement. Show me how many lawsuits you're involved in, show me how much money you have in the bank." So we got into a partnership without me seeing everything, and the next thing I do is I look up and I'm in bed with a couple of criminals; they're in a bunch of trouble. I had to disconnect from them. And when I disconnected from them, they sued me, and it was an ugly deal. I trusted without proof, it was lazy.

Takeaway: Always have people show, not tell.

GRANT CARDONE'S

12

COMMANDMENTS

HOW TO MAKE
MILLIONS IN
BUSINESS

1

Go to market directly

Don't sit around and plan, organize, and play with your new computer. Get to market! Remember that speed is power. Urgency is divine. Be the tortoise AND the hare. People plan too much and do too little.

2

Promote like a maniac

Blow your freaking horn. Be loud, let people know you exist. If they don't know you they'll never buy from you. Tell people you are the greatest. Believe it and be it.

3

Make sales your Divine Inspiration

Sales is where money is. Get great at sales and you'll get great amounts of money. Sell or be sold.

4

Do it before you delegate it

Do things yourself before you ask others to. I've done everything and I'm not afraid to get my hands dirty. No job is beneath me and you need to be willing to do whatever it takes.

5

Brand before you advertise

You have to know who you are and what you stand for before going out in the market place. Like I said earlier, find clarity in your pitch. The better people know you the more receptive they'll be to your message. Stay consistent with your brand.

6

Cash flow is the Holy Grail

Cash is king as I've preached to you so much. You need money coming in from lots of places every month. Without cash flow you can't grow big and you'll instead flat line and go out of business.

7

Create multiple parallel flows

If you have one flow and that faucet turns off you've got nothing. I've created multiple companies and you'll need to do the same.

8

Stay broke

Don't be a baller when you're middle class at best. I didn't buy expensive watches or cars until I had paid the price. Keep shoving money aside until you can invest it.

9

Stay hungry

Being smart is great but I'll take a hustler any day. You don't learn hustle at Harvard. Stay hungry and don't get satisfied.

10

Beat up new technology and throw it away

I made Twitter my b*tch, now I'm making SnapChat my new one. Technology will come and go so use it and lose it.

11

Expand while others run away

Growth is where it's at. Get big or go home. Be massive or be passive.

12

Fire to grow

If you're not growing, fire someone. Perform or get out. NFL clubs don't keep losing coaches for long. Why should you?

Business Successes

1. Million dollar decision
2. Promote first and promote big
3. Make sales your divine inspiration
4. Deliver more than promised.
5. Immerse your client in products.
6. Replace every client with new leads
7. Reinvest cash flow

Takeaway: Use this simple formula to guide you to expansion.

"STAYING POOR IS SELFISH."

– Grant Cardone

10X BEASTMODE 24-HOUR CLOCK

1. 168 HOURS / WEEK
2. 5840 HOURS / WAKE
3. 8760 HOURS / TOTAL

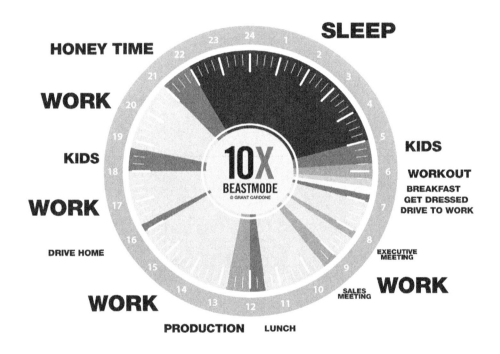

Average Employee

- Works 1,750 hours per year
- Makes $52,000 a year
- Earns $29.70 per hour

The way to buy time is to hire people. Even if this guy only works 1,750 hours, if I have 5 people, I buy myself a total of 8,750 hours. You guys out there worried about hiring people, remember, 22 million small businesses in America have no employees. None, zero, why? Because the middle-class thing is hammered around that business owner saying, "Don't hire anybody." People don't cost money. 8,750 hours times $30 bucks, that's money but what are you losing by not doing it? 8,750 hours. If these people aren't productive, what do I need to do? Get rid of them as fast as I possibly can.

Takeaway: Buying time is expensive, but losing time might be more expensive.

Triple Your Income

- Work 5,250 hours per year instead of 1750
- Earn $156,000 instead of $52,000
- $29.70 per hour

Takeaway: You want to make more? Do more work.

If Time is Money Then Buy Time

- ME   4,500 Hours
- EMPLOYEES   73,500 Hours
- PRODUCTIVITY   78,000 Hours

Takeaway: Do the math when it comes to productivity and buying time.

TIPS TO SUCCEED IN BUSINESS

"What you have done is nothing compared to what you can do"
– Grant Cardone

HOW TO MAKE MILLIONS IN BUSINESS

Tips To Succeed in Business

Measure everything and make adjustments fast. Everything should be measured. In my real estate division, we're looking at numbers all the time and I try to improve those numbers. We have these graphs and we look at them and I can see what's up, what's down, and why? Why is it down? Why is there an aberration here? Why has something dropped? Why did something go up?

Look, it's about being a business. This is not a lot of work. I'm going to tell you what's more work. Staying small is a lot of work. It takes a tremendous effort. Try this tomorrow—drive to work with your foot on the break the entire time. That's what people are doing in business. Their foot's on the break. If you want to really know what people are doing, drive backwards the next day to work because that's what most people are doing. They're just going backwards from some other experience that they had.

Takeaway: Measure your progress—or lack thereof.

Tips To Succeed in Business

- ## Your Decisions Determine Everything.

Put a stake in the ground and make a decision. Your decisions are going to determine your outcomes in life. Don't make them lightly but also don't spend too much time on them. Sometimes you just need to make a decision and get on with things.

Takeaway: Make quick decisions but make them wisely.

Tips To Succeed in Business

• Promote before you Advertise.

Promotion is easy to get implemented and a great deal less expensive than blowing deals. Start promotion early and your advertising will pay off later. You want people to already be hearing about you before they hear your ad.

Takeaway: Don't worry about advertising right now, concentrate on promoting yourself and getting known—even being omnipresent.

Tips To Succeed in Business

• Sales Cure All

I believe success is my duty and I show up every day in the marketplace to win. I want to be a threat in the marketplace. I want my competition to feel my presence. I want to be the king of my space. I have to be bold. I have to take chances. I must have an opinion. And guess what – I believe you must too. Whatever problems you have in business, sales will cure it. There is nothing that helps a business more than new sales.

Takeaway: At the end of the day it's all about sales.

Tips To Succeed in Business

- ## Deliver more than you promised and promise a lot

The GREATS promise their clients a lot and then over deliver on what they promise. Do you remember the old saying, "under promise and over deliver?" Don't subscribe to this idea. Know that you have to OVER promise AND over deliver. Be exceptional. Look to commit big and deliver even bigger. This is what it takes:

- Make big claims.
- Let people know you're the best
- Let people know you're the best price
- Let people know you have the superior product
- Let people know you're the most affordable

Takeaway: Over-promise but also over-deliver.

New Millionaires Every Day

You need to decide to get rich and get rid of any remaining poverty think. Poverty think concentrates on how much something costs rather than what the potential benefit would be. Poor people worry about the cost of a $30 book while rich people think about the value that can be gained with the knowledge in that $30 book.

Think about benefits and abundance, not costs and shortages. New Millionaires are made each day. It's time for you to join the group.

Takeaway: Be a millionaire!

Questions:
How to Make Millions in Business

1. You don't start a business, you _____ a business.

2. Business ____/20.

3. What part of your business shouldn't take more than 20 seconds?

4. Can you hire new employees without cash flow?

5. What percentage of small businesses in America make less than $25,000 a year?

6. Can you name Grant Cardone's 12 Commandments?

From 1 Million to Wealth

I've stated several times that a million dollars isn't what it used to be. If you want wealth, you will need more than a million dollars. That's why I created the Wealth Creation Formula.

There are people who get rich quick but nobody gets wealthy quick. Soak in this material until you know it by heart. It's a formula that works—I use it, and if you use it you, too can be wealthy. Money won't make you happy, but being broke won't bring happiness eit her, so you might as well have some money to go with your unhapp iness.

Better yet, be positive.

Being broke sucks, but remain positive no matter what your condition currently is. At my office, I have a no negativity allowed policy. Negativity isn't just complaining about the weather or how you didn't enjoy your lunch. Negative comments can come in many different forms. "That is impossible", "That's not my job", "I can't do that" etc. will only bring you and others down.

Commit to staying positive and let's get you on the wealth creatio n formula!

Course 4

I'm proud to be introducing my wealth creation formula, which comes from my thirty plus years of studying the wealthy and then codifying how to use those strategies to create wealth in my own life. Use this formula to get rich. It worked for me and it will work for you if you apply it. - Grant

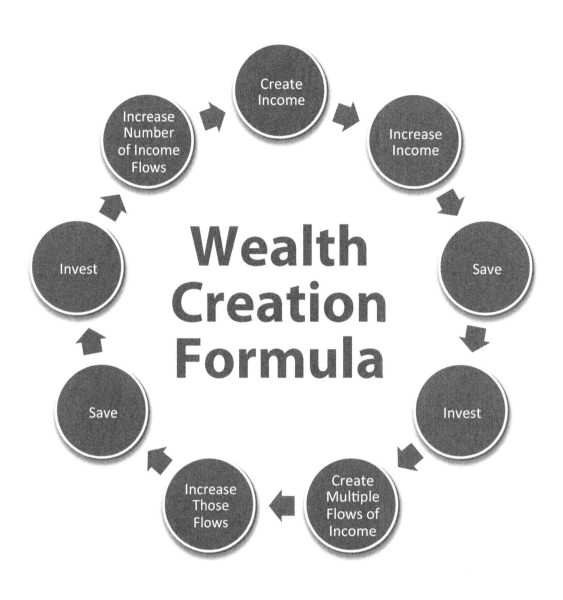

Wealth Creation Formula

- Create Income
- Increase Income
- Save
- Invest
- Create Multiple Flows of Income
- Increase Those Flows
- Save
- Invest
- Increase Number of Income Flows

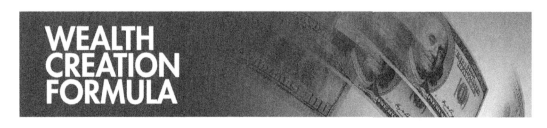

WEALTH CREATION FORMULA

Step 1:
Create Income

Despite what anyone tells you, it is impossible to get rich without income. It cannot happen.

Yes, there are things that make income less attractive than other ways to create wealth. Income is basically the money you earn from a job, or the money that comes from a stock—possibly called dividend income. The reason a lot of people say income is the least desired method is because it is the most heavily taxed.

The reality is you aren't going to get away from it. The whole game is rigged. But if you understand the entire wealth creation formula you can get the game to work in your favor. Just know the game is rigged. The entry to the game is income—there's no way around it.

The question is: what can you do right now to increase income?

Takeaway: You cannot become wealthy without first increasing income.

Step 1:
Create Income *(Continued)*

Let's say you don't have a job. We all start without a job.

What can you do without a job to create income today? The first thing, number o ne, is to have a target for your income. Let's say my daughter, six-year-old Sabri na, wants to create wealth now. I can't send her to college, she's 6. Why woul d I wait 10-12 years? You understand I want her to create wealth NOW. Our syst em, remember I told you it was rigged? Well what they tell you is, "You want to ge t a job? Go get a degree from college."

That's ridiculous.

You don't need to go to college to get a job or get income. To start from zero, no money in the bank, no investments, you need income—not student debt. You need a strategy and a formula. Nowhere in the steps of the Wealth Creation Formula does it say: Go to college.

Takeaway: College is not the way to start your path to wealth.

Step 1:
Create Income *(Continued)*

It doesn't matter if you make $10k or $400k a year, you need income first.

You could be in poverty, you could be making $30,000 a year with a family of four, you could be a single mother making $19k or maybe most or all of your money comes from the government. We all start from somewhere. Maybe you're in the middle class. Maybe you only have enough money left each month to go to the movies and have dinner once—and if you go twice you won't be able to make your bills on time.

Maybe you're making between $70k and $110k a year and have been for a while. You're better off than those in your neighborhood. You have a better car, you don't worry about bills, you don't worry about new clothes for your kids—but you never have quite enough to make a big play to push into a wealth position.

You feel like you're never going to get rich.

No matter how much income you have, unless you have created all the steps you are in Step One: Creating Income—it's the front door. You MUST walk through it.

Takeaway: No matter what, you cannot skip Step One: Create Income.

Step 1:
Create Income *(Continued)*

You need to learn to create revenue... and then get even better at it.

I create more revenue in shorter periods of time now compared to in the past. I first had to learn to create revenue—and then I got better at it. Income is your first step, your entry, your front door.

You must fortify this thing and make it strong. You have to add value to what you do to make it bigger and you even if you hate your job—or your current position in life—never complain about the income. No matter how small it is, how dirty your hands have to get, don't complain. I've done jobs I hate. I still do jobs today I hate. I never complain about them.

Never complain about the job you have. Your job is creating income and making sure you have a job that will be there for you tomorrow. Once you've made sure of that, fortify it and make sure you cannot be replaced by some piece of technology or new employee. Make sure you become that person the organization you are with wants to continue to send income.

All wealth starts with this front door right here—income.

Takeaway: Learn how to create revenue and then fortify it.

Step 2:
Increase Income

Once you have begun to create income your only concern should be to increase your income.

The only thing you should care about is, "How do I increase this income I created from this first job?" It doesn't say to get a second job, a third job or a fourth job. It says to increase the income of the first stream you created. Get it?

Whether you are mowing lawns or selling stocks as this first stream of income, once you have fortified this income don't go start a new business. Don't look for a second flow elsewhere. Make your first flow bigger, make it juicier, I want you to increase the intensity of it. Don't even worry about saving right now—all you want to do is get a job and increase that income flow.

Takeaway: Increase the first flow, don't look for a second.

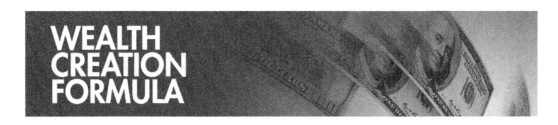

Step 2:
Increase Income *(Continued)*

Don't get caught up in a business plan, just follow the steps.

Back to the example of my daughter: One time I taught her how to get money from Stephen G. She asked him, "What do I have to do for you to pay me a hundred dollars?" Remember, she's six. Stephen says, "I need you to run five laps." Excellent! She runs five laps and says, "I did that fast—how about a tip? How about a little bonus for speed?"

You have to understand, she first created wealth asking how to make a hundred, fortified it by accomplishing the job and then pushed to increase the income from that task, that job.

Don't worry about a business plan. You need to first create income so that if you need to go to the bank later you can show how much income you made—because sooner or later they are going to ask. And it's like this all along the Wealth Creation Formula. As you take steps along the wheel you create, fortify and increase. You don't branch off, skip, or go in a different order. Step one is to create income and step two is to increase income.

Takeaway: It's simple if you stop over-complicating what I'm telling you.

Step 2:
Increase Income *(Continued)*

Don't become satisfied with your first income flow.

Once you get your income your second job is to increase that income. Now if you're satisfied, which is what happens to most people, you're misinformed—which is how the system wants you to be. Remember, it's rigged.

Most people are satisfied because they are comparing their situation to someone else's and that's where they stop. They stop their wealth creation once they have surpassed someone else's situation in life and then wonder why they never become wealthy.

You never get wealthy creating one income flow and never increasing that income. Think of it like water. You're at an oasis, you drink and get one bottle. You think you're fine, you're hydrated and that's good so you go on your way. Then another guy comes by and drinks and fills up a bottle, then waters his camel and fills up that bottle again and again before leaving. He knows when he's further on he won't have access to that oasis. And you go to take a sip and your one bottle already went empty miles back... and now you're thirsty again.

Don't depend on one flow that never increases.

Takeaway: Don't let your wealth depend on one income flow that never increases.

Step 3:
Save It All

This is what separates the haves from the have nots.

Step 3 of the Wealth Creation Formula is to save it all. Okay, you went from making $45k a year to $60k or $60k to $80k or maybe you went from making $0 a week to $200 a week. Now you save it all—and understand this is how I created wealth.

Maybe you're mowing grass for $200 a week. That's step one, create the income. Then the second step is to increase the income. Get more lawns to mow in the same amount of time, so you learn to mow lawns faster. Compress your time.

Then you start realizing you can increase your income—it becomes real when you start making the money. You start to imagine going from $200 a week to $1400 to $6000 and now you have a little business going. So you expand to a landscaping business. Now you're dominating the market.

You'll never get there if you don't save—you'll be broke forever and working harder than when you were at zero.

Takeaway: You won't get to wealth without saving it all.

Step 3:
Save It All *(Continued)*

Save for the big play. You won't make it to wealth without sacrifice.

Up until this point you've been struggling so you won't be sacrificing much anyway. You need to keep living at the same standards. Don't buy anything new, no new debt unless it brings you positive return. Your clothes won't change. Don't buy a big watch. You want to operate so to the world it still looks like you are broke—but keep stacking that money away.

The trick I did from the age of 25 to 36 was I rated my expenditures from 1 to 5. Look at your bank account, look at your checkbook. Go over the last 30 days and rate everything from 1 to 5. 1 means its necessary, 3 means it's a maybe, and 4 and 5 you didn't need. If you have something around the house that's a 4 or 5 take it back to the store. Return it. Get your money back and save it. Now you're back to Step 2: Increasing Income.

Sacrifice the trips to Starbucks, the extra pairs of shoes, too many movie nights, all these things that won't build you wealth. Pay the price today so you can pay any price tomorrow. You want to be the guy or girl at the table who can cover the whole tab without even thinking about it.

Takeaway: Rate your purchases from 1 to 5. Remove the things you don't need.

Step 3:
Save It All *(Continued)*

Be a miser early in the process if you want surges and spikes in wealth.

If you want a real shot at huge, giant, MASSIVE surges and spikes in wealth you must be willing to save it all in the meantime. It sounds tough, and it is, but it's worth it. Once you start seeing your savings hitting levels you've never had before you'll realize the value of the sacrifice. Even if you don't trust yourself right now that's okay. I couldn't trust myself at 25 that's why I invested in training and followed it without question until I knew how to make decisions on my own—which took years of confidence and discipline.

You have to squeeze down, manage and control your money. Most people don't know how to make money. Fewer people know how to keep it. The reason why is they only keep tiny little pieces. Why do you want to increase your income if you're just going to get rid of most of it?

Don't spend all week killing yourself to earn money, sacrificing time with your family, just to blow your paycheck drinking over the weekend. The system is rigged for this. How simple is it to blow your paycheck at the bar? How complicated is it to learn about wealth-creating investments? You have to hire a 'professional' to manage your money it's so complex... but you don't need to hire someone to show you how to drink your money away. It's simple and it keeps people broke and struggling.

Takeaway: You won't see surges in income until you become a miser.

Step 4:
Invest

Most people move to this step prematurely and end up broke.

You've been told to invest in little pieces, here and there and to diversify your portfolio—this is all wrong. This is a part of the system that holds people back from real wealth. You don't want to start with little and end up with little. You want to make HUGE moves and for that you need to make HUGE investments. You need to know what you're doing with what you invest in.

The only reason to save money is to invest money. Your parents didn't tell you that part. They were taught to save money just to save so they could hope to maintain a 'quality of living' when they got old. How has that worked out for them? Nearly 29% aged 55 and up don't have retirement savings or a traditional pension plan. They saved to save, they didn't save to invest and the return got them nowhere.

You are putting money away to make surges in wealth, to multiply money. The first thing you must do is commit to money. You must say, "I want to be wealthy!"

Takeaway: You won't create wealth without learning how to invest.

Step 4:
Invest *(Continued)*

If you invest for a rainy day you'll be broke when a meteor hits.

If you want money you must commit to wealth, commit to wealth with your family and friendships, commit to wealth in your relationships, commit to wealth with your brand, commit to wealth your community, and commit to wealth with your business.

"You aren't a businessman, you're a business, man." – Jay Z

How do you do that with investing? Expend money with the expectation of achieving a profit or material result. Don't just throw it in a 401k or IRA—by the time you have any real value there you will be old. You can't easily reinvest it. It's no good.

You need to setup financial schemes. Yes, scheme, which the dictionary defines as, a "large-scale systematic plan or arrangement for attaining some particular object or putting a particular idea into effect." You do this with property investments or developing a business venture.

There are only two reasons to have money: 1) buy essentials, and 2) invest to create new money. Money was invented because it's easier to carry around and trade at the market than a goat or a chicken.

Takeaway: You must commit to wealth and investing to grow money.

Step 4:
Invest *(Continued)*

But how do I take little to no money and become wealthy?

This program is about creating wealth from no money, but you will never get wealthy if you do not save to invest. There are two reasons people don't become wealthy: 1) they never earned any real amount of money, and 2) they never invested big enough amounts in big enough investments.

Look at all the NBA players who make unbelievable amounts of money and have none of it once they stop playing. They file for bankruptcy, they are broke after years of making millions and millions of dollars. They never learned how to invest to expand their wealth. They expended money they didn't expand their money. You must expand your money with the expectation of achieving a profit to take that money and make it bigger.

That's the only goal of saving, the only reason to save it all.

Takeaway: Don't expend your money, expand it.

Step 4:

Invest *(Continued)*

You are never too old or too young to start saving to invest.

Whether you're 25 years old, 45 years old or 55 years it's not too late and it doesn't matter what level you are at. If you're broke, starting from zero, have $10k in the bank, $100k in the bank or you have a million to invest—you aren't going to go bigger without saving to invest and you must only invest when you KNOW the market you're investing in.

Most people invest too early, not too late. What I mean is they invest with pennies and nickels because they haven't set aside a big chunk to invest in something. If you invest pennies and nickels you're only going to get pennies and nickels in return—I want to get gold bars the size of trucks from my investments. I want wealth so massive no situation on Earth could take away from it.

The big players on this planet invested all-in with what they believed in. Railroads, the automobile, the cellphone... all of these were HUGE investments of time, energy and money and they didn't mess with anything else until that first investment was so big they had money to play around with.

Takeaway: Stop thinking with limitations for your future wealth.

Step 5:
Create Multiple Flows

You aren't going to have secure wealth without multiple flows of income.

Like I said before, you can have one HUGE massive flow of income, like an NBA player or a CEO with no other sources of income. What happens when that dries up? How many flows do you need for multiple flows? Two, six, thirty four, five? Remember, no target no success. You can't hit a goal that doesn't exist.

It is said, and I haven't researched this, that the average millionaire has 7 flows of income. I don't depend on 7 flows and I wouldn't suggest you should either, but you can't just jump from 1 to 7 or more—I just know you can't depend on 1 and expect to get anywhere with your wealth.

And remember, I'm not just talking about money—wealth to me is a collection of things. It could be money, friends, fans on Facebook, books written, or the accumulation of information. I want a wealth of information, a wealth of mentors, a wealth of supporters—you get the idea.

Takeaway: You cannot depend on one flow of income to make it BIG.

Step 5:
Create Multiple Flows (Continued)

Your first flows of income must be symbiotic.

The dictionary defines symbiotic as, "having an interdependent relationship." What that means here is that once you have one flow you don't go make a second flow somewhere else in another company, for another business or with something that isn't like your first flow.

For me I worked a sales job. I got paid $250 every week. I did Step 1: Create Income, but I couldn't become wealthy making $250 a week so I had to figure out how to fortify that. I worked commission so I had to learn how to get our product successfully into the hands of someone who wanted it—more sales meant more income. I increased my income from $250 a week to $2,500 and my confidence exploded. I now understood how economies worked and I kept living like I was making $250 a week. Steps 1, 2 and 3.

So I have to do Step 4: Invest , so I invest in making myself better at sales. I invest in training and personal growth. I wasn't ready to make big investments in real estate yet, I didn't know enough. So I get to Step 5: Create Multiple Flows. Here's where things started to speed up. I had to find a second flow that went with my first flow—sales. So I started helping with financing deals. I started to bring in more leads and take them to the service department and the repair department. Instead of the company paying outside people to bring in leads they started to pay me to bring leads to different departments. A second flow symbiotic to the first. I didn't go anywhere and it helped my first flow grow.

Takeaway: Your flows must work together to make each flow stronger.

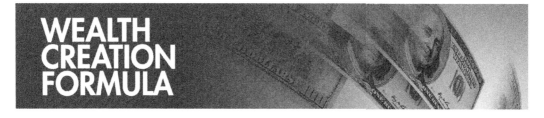

Step 5:
Create Multiple Flows *(Continued)*

Keep your multiple flows within 3 feet of you. You must be able to control the space around you before you can go wide.

This company I started bringing leads to sold warranties as well, so I asked if I could bring them leads for that and what happened?—another flow of income. I looked into referrals and made buddies with the other people I competed with—I couldn't sell every customer so I gave them to my competition for a referral fee. That way I could make money on any lead, sold, unsold, another department, anywhere that lead went I got a flow.

Then I started buying our product and selling it from home. Now I'm 25 with my base income, my commission, my service leads, financing, referrals, buying and reselling the product—one place and now I have around 7 flows of income. All from different sources but all from the same location. I didn't have to go anywhere else for all this. I'm up to like 12 hours a day. I didn't get a second job, a third or fourth job. Seven flows with only one job.

What's the point of all this? Control the 3 feet around you before you go out and try to conquer the world. You need to be able to dominate your space before you can go out. You need to fortify that first flow and build your other flows next to it.

You need symbiotic, parallel income flows.

Takeaway: Can you get more than 3 flows where you work now?

Step 6:
Increase Those Flows

Almost everybody has two or three flows to start with. Look at every flow you have.

Most people incorrectly think they only have one flow of income—their job. Do you have a savings account? That pays dividends, no matter how small—that's a second flow, so make sure to consider them income flows. You must fully understand what flows of income you have so you can increase them rather than chasing new income flows.

What do you do to increase these flows? Well, with that savings account you can't go ask the bank to pay you more in dividends, so what can you do? You could take that money and lend it out; that would be one way to do it. You have to be creative, but smart. Don't just throw your money into anything just because it's exciting. That's how you go broke.

You have to properly identify the flows you have so you can increase them properly. Money goes to the things you put attention on. Put attention on your flows of income so you can increase them.

Takeaway: How many flows of income do you really have?

WEALTH CREATION FORMULA

Step 6:
Increase Those Flows *(Continued)*

You have to get into sales.

So now you have a couple flows going, two, three, five, seven... as long as they are symbiotic you are going in the right direction. If you're at 40 income flows we'll talk about that later. So now what can you do to increase those flows?

Sales. We're talking about the increase of revenue.

Mark Cuban says you must learn sales if you're going to be in business. When we're talking about how Warren Buffett evaluates a company based on revenue and how the company manages revenue—again we're talking about sales.

- Communication
- Motivation
- Branding
- Marketing
- Going Wide

Takeaway: You must get into sales to increase your flows and go wide.

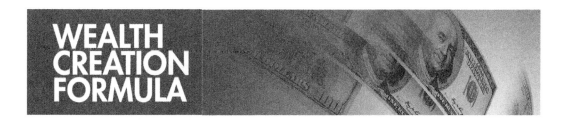

Step 6:
Increase Those Flows *(Continued)*

This is not the stage where you worry about making products better.

We are talking about your value as an individual here. Your ability to create revenue in the marketplace, your value at your job—it's based on your ability to create revenue at your post: manager, executive, company owner, investment shareholder... your value in the company is to bring in revenue.

Even if you're a philanthropist or running a charity, say you run the Red Cross, your value is not to organize the Red Cross or make the Red Cross do more. Your value is to bring in more revenue so the Red Cross can do more great things—focus on the revenue. Commit first, figure the rest out later.

How do you bring in more money every waking moment while at work or with your family? Your wealth creation should be flowing with your spouse, your kids, your company, your department—you want everyone around you thinking about increasing revenue.

Takeaway: Don't try to reinvent the wheel—learn how to sell the wheel to more people faster.

Step 6:
Increase Those Flows *(Continued)*

Revenue can solve all product problems. Put all your attention on it.

Who's got the money to fund my projects? Who can help me hit my targets? What are my targets? How many units do I have to sell to hit that target? You must keep attention on this. What's the target for my department with this product or service?

Who do I have to make contact with on each of these flows? Evaluate each flow constantly, looking at the flows and how they can go wider and wider. I'm telling you what I was doing when I was twenty-eight, twenty-nine and thirty. I didn't own the company I worked at. I've increased my flows. I've started to invest a little in my 3 foot space that I talked about earlier. I'm just trying to make those bigger. Those investments are flows and I want to increase those flows.

Now what am I doing every month, every week, every day to make those bigger and better? I'm looking at my targets. Every day I write my targets down—when I wake up and again before I go to sleep. Over 700 times a year my attention is directly on my goals. I'm looking at my checking account, I'm looking at my savings account, I'm looking at my sacred accounts, I'm looking at my customers, I'm looking at my time, I'm looking at my appointments... I'm keeping my attention on everything that is a flow. All of it.

Takeaway: "Who's Got My Money?"

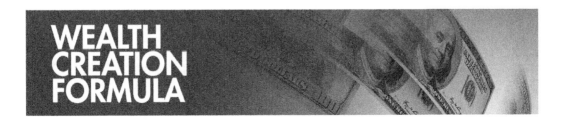

Step 7:
Save Some More

Don't crap out.
This is different than saving in step 3.

Saving here is very different than earlier in the Wealth Creation Formula. You might have gone from $0 in the bank to $18,000. I remember the first time I saved my first $18k, I was like, "Oh my gosh! I have eighteen-thousand dollars!" A salesperson who worked with me also saved $18k, but he went out and blew his money and had to start over again from zero. If you want to stop hitting zero and starting over you must do what I did. All I did with my money was invest in myself, only myself. Remember the three foot rule from earlier.

Early on there is no money to make big investments for surges. Early on your focus is to create income and increase those flows. Keep putting that money away. Sooner or later you are going to look up and that $18k is going to be $50k, $100k or even $250k if you stay disciplined and focus on CREATING money, not spending it.

Don't make big plays yet. You aren't ready for that yet, even if you've saved $250k.

Takeaway: Don't try to make big plays yet. Focus on saving.

Step 7:
Save Some More *(Continued)*

You want to build lifeboats so when the ship goes down you are ready.

Having one-million dollars in the bank does not make you stress free. It puts you exactly into anxiety. You know the value of money and have some put away but can lose it all with one bad investment. Don't get ahead of your wealth and begin bragging—don't become a pretender spender. That fancy car didn't get you all that money in the bank, the watch didn't get you a flow of income... stick with what is working—saving money in sacred accounts.

Maybe your lifeboat is a savings account that you have unlimited check writing ability on, but the reality is you don't want to write checks out of this account. You could use a checking account. I like to use Money Market accounts with a limitation of one or two checks a month. These accounts are sacred and shouldn't be touched until you have $100,000 or more in them. Don't even think about them as available until they are over $1 million. Keep your attention on saving and putting those flows into these sacred accounts. Only make investments in yourself—because it gives you a positive return on the investment that you can control.

Build your lifeboats and have multiple lifeboats.

Takeaway: Keep putting money away until you are over $1,000,000.

Step 7:
Save Some More *(Continued)*

It doesn't take money to make money, it takes courage.

I know people with a lot of money who do not have the courage to use the money. I had over a million dollars in my sacred accounts before I put some of it at risk. My living standards hadn't changed from when I was at $0 and now I'm at $1,000,000. It was tough to not go out and spend money but every time I looked at my account getting bigger I realized the sacrifice was worth it—paying the price today so I can pay any price tomorrow.

Right here you are planning to reach out past that three feet of control—and it's scary. I want everything I put my money in so close I can touch it; I want everything parallel and under control because I've never been a lucky guy. I've never had a tremendous amount of courage for taking risk and it always feels like I have to work harder than most people. If you can relate, then you understand why at this point in the Wealth Creation Formula you must save and wait for the big play.

Be extremely conservative. I didn't make my first big investment until I had over $1,000,000 in my sacred accounts.

Takeaway: Save until you have a real play available.

Step 8:
Invest in Your Big Deal

This is where you get rich folks. This is where you make the big play.

Like I mentioned earlier you need to expand money, not just expend it. By definition an investment is, "the action or process of investing money for profit or material result." You need to take your money and put it into a scheme. A scheme is, "a large-scale systematic plan or arrangement for attaining some particular object or putting a particular idea into effect." It's actually something very, very positive—but how many of you thought it was something negative?

So here you are making the big play, you're investing in a scheme. Will it be a business, will it be real estate, will it be the stock market? I don't like the stock market. There's a lot to know about investments and this space can be confusing. If it's something I can wrap my head around and it's simple I'm good. If I cannot understand it I will not touch it. Keep that in mind.

Takeaway: If you cannot wrap your head around it, do not invest in it.

Step 8:
Invest in Your Big Deal

(Continued)

There are three types of investments to look at: Big Bang, Dividend, or Both.

When I look at an investment I'm looking at three possibilities. Big Bang, I'm just keeping the language simple here—remember, if I don't understand it I don't invest in it—and the big bang is an explosion on the return. The second one is a Dividend or cash flow. For example, I made an investment in real estate of $10,000 and I make $100 a month or $1,200 a year on that—the dividend is $1,200 a year.

I look for the third group: Both—something that is explosive and gives a dividend.

I like both. I like the flow of dividends because I'm an insecure financial person and I like to see a little drip, a little nibble on my fishing line which means a little income every month with the chance that I catch a big one.

Criteria for an investment:

1. It has to be a sure thing.
2. I need to know what I'm doing. If I can't explain it to someone else, I don't get it.
3. Make sure it can never be destroyed.

"Rule No.1: Never lose money. Rule No.2: Never forget rule No.1." - Warren Buffett

Takeaway: Understand the 3 types of investments.

Step 8:
Invest in Your Big Deal
(Continued)

Your investment must be a sure thing, you have to know what you're doing and it can't be able to be disrupted.

Coca-Cola was founded in 1892. Warren Buffett owns 9.2% of that multi-billion dollar company. For him it's a sure thing, Coca-Cola isn't going away. He knows what he's doing when he invests in it. When he looks around he sees people drinking the soda, their billboards and commercials are everywhere. When the economy turns down people still consume Coca-Cola products—it's a sure thing and it can't be disrupted.

He's also got money in Walmart, Wells Fargo, Kraft, Heinz, Apple, Procter & Gamble, American Express. You know all of these company names because they are a part of every day life. And don't look at this like diversifying—Warren Buffett is to a point of wealth where he can expand and create multiple flows like this. You should be looking for ONE sure thing.

Each investment you make must be like this. You must know it's a sure thing and if it isn't don't play around and gamble with it—if you want to gamble go to a casino and don't expect to make money.

Your investments need to pay you in dividends so they become new drips, new flows of income that you can add into your Wealth Creation Formula.

Takeaway: Only invest in a sure thing that cannot be disrupted.

Step 9:
Increase Number of Income Flows

Don't forget the first flows. Here you should be increasing all your flows and increasing the number of flows.

This step is for those who want to get to ridiculous amounts of wealth. This is where the biggest players play. They're never satisfied and they're always trying to create more flows. Some of you might think they are greedy, but these are the people giving out all the money. These are the people building hospitals and bridges and leaving their legacies for generations after they die.

You might not end up putting your name on a hospital but this kind of wealth is available to you if you want it. Now more than any time in history, you can grow to this place of wealth. You don't need to be born into money or invent the next best thing.

I created the Wealth Creation Formula to pass on this kind of wealth to you. I don't want to be destroyed at the end of my life. I want my legacy to live on and your legacy to live on—and that legacy needs to be funded. You won't have a legacy for being broke or making $1,000,000. Nearly 500,000 new millionaires were created in the U.S. alone in 2014... no one will know who they are. You must get SUPER wealthy to leave a legacy.

Takeaway: Will you leave a legacy and become super wealthy?

Step 9:
Increase Number of Income Flows *(Continued)*

Keep your main thing your main thing.

I had five or six little drips going, plus my savings accounts so I decided to quit my job to go into business for myself. I went from all those drips down to one, my savings account—plus now I have to actually pay people who work for me, for the office space, the office equipment and on and on. This is why most people move backwards when they are catching speed—they forget their main thing.

Remember, 80% of millionaires work for someone else—that means only 20% of them went out and made it on their own to become millionaires. Think back about what I said on knowing it's a sure thing. Which is better, 80% or 20%?

Takeaway: 80% of millionaires in 2015 work for someone else.

Step 9:
Increase Number of Income Flows *(Continued)*

You have to grow and expand as you get around this circle of steps.

This isn't Step 5 or Step 6. At this point you aren't at $0 or $10k in your sacred accounts. This is the big Step 9 where you are looking for surges like Step 8.

How do you build wealth at this level? You build your brand. How do you build your wealth at this level? You build value. You must be doing all this with a purpose. You aren't going to get super wealthy without a purpose—and if you're just doing it to get rich you've already lost interest a few steps ago. Once you can go on vacation, stop worrying about car payments and take care of your kids you'll lose interest in going wider, making even bigger plays and becoming super wealthy—unless you have a bigger purpose.

My purpose is to help 7 billion people on this planet. That's why, "Success is my duty, obligation and responsibility." This is my purpose this is what keeps me going, fighting for more, keeps me hungry and hunting no matter what I stack away. I want to leave a legacy. I want people to know Grant Cardone and how I helped people get real financial freedom in their lives—helped them realize they can help the entire planet. Wealth is about more than money.

Be great. Nothing else pays... much.

Takeaway: Are you doing this with a purpose or just going after money?

Questions:
Wealth Creation Formula

1. What is it impossible to get rich without?

2. Don't worry about the _____ plan.

3. Have you gone back and rated your recent purchases from 1 to 5?

4. Do most invest too early or too late?

5. Write down your current flows of income here:

6. Only make investments in _____, because it gives you a positive return on the investment that you can control.

Sales Assist in Wealth Creation

I am a salesman because I had to be, not because I wanted to be. Truth be told I hated sales when I got into it. I hear people say, "you are a natural salesman." Wrong. I am the most unnatural sales person you would ever meet and hated sales the first 8 years I was in it.

At the age of 17 on my first sales job in a clothing store my card said, 'sales associate' and I hated it. I hated talking to strangers, "is there something I can help you with?" I was awkward, often tongue-tied, scared to approach people, hated rejection and my results relied purely on luck. My results relied on whether I met the right customer or not—or so I thought. I got in sales because my survival depended on it, not because I wanted to. The career that had been set for me didn't pay any money. Sales was the only job offered to me and I hated it. I told my uncle, "I didn't go to college to become a salesman." And he said, "You didn't go to college to be out of work either." So I took the sales job and for the next two years I hated it. I hated building rapport with a customer, asking probing questions, and hated asking for the offer. Hate is not too strong of a word. I hated the ups and downs, the commission only, the rejection, appointments not showing, customers lying to me...and the begging and follow up it seemed I was expected to do. The point is you don't need to like sales—you need to understand your entire future depends on it and quit fighting it. Very few people inherently like sales. Everyone I know who loves sales loves it because they are successful at it.

In 25 years I have never met a person in sales that loves it that is failing at it. I have met a lot of sales people that do love their profession and they all have two things in common—they make money and they KNOW what they are doing.

Course 5

I have helped thousands of salespeople over the years learn to fall in love with their career and it is my experience that to really love sales and make a lot of money doing it, two things must happen. 1) Commit to it as your survival. You don't need to want to do it, love to do it, or even like to do it—that will come when you get results. You must commit to it with no other options. 2) Learn how to do it. Even if you were born a salesperson, whatever that means, then you will have to learn it step by step. By the way, I know lots of people I grew up with who felt like they were born salespeople and I sold circles around them once I learned the game.

TOP SALES SECRETS

It All Starts with YOU

"No product, price, economy, education or amount of money matters more than you." - GC

Always, always, always be prepared. Nowhere else is this truer than in the world of sales. Be prepared for EVERY possible question, objection, stall, obstacle, delay, and customer question possible. Every time I ever hear something new from a client that I have not heard before, I write it down and then in my private time I prepare a number of responses that I can use in the future to help me handle that situation the next time I hear it. It starts with me—and for you it starts with you.

Takeaway: You can't get away from the work of preparation.

Pre-Tip 1
Decide to Be GREAT

Not even magic will make you better in sales until you decide to be great. The average salesperson is average not because of a lack of skills but a lack of commitment. The sales strategies I will share with you today are extremely powerful but they will not work without your commitment to being great.

I have worked with tens of thousands of salespeople and the biggest problem 80% of them face is there is no commitment to greatness. The best sales strategies will not work without your willingness and commitment to greatness. Decide now to be the best in your industry, not just the best at your company. Quit focusing on how you compare to others around you and make a commitment to become the example of every salesperson in your industry.

After fooling around with sales for 5 years, I finally committed to becoming great at it. I quit comparing myself to those immediately around me and made a serious commitment to becoming great as a professional salesperson. I invested the resources, energy and time it took to become great. I watched video instruction, listened to audio programming and role played everyday to follow up my commitment.

Takeaway: You are just one decision away from everything you've ever wanted.

Deny Your Reality
Sell to Your Potential

Most salespeople only sell to their existing reality, problems, economic conditions, inventory, standards set by others or their quota. After I made a commitment to becoming great and then followed that up everyday with training, I no longer accepted a quota by a manager. I started looking at what I was capable of, not just what I was doing. I quit comparing myself to others and started getting real with myself.

Let me give you an example of comparing reality to potential. People work 35 hours a week because that is their reality. The potential of work available is 113 hours if you sleep 8 hours a night. When you deny your reality you will quit making excuses for not achieving your potential. Sell to your potential and let go of all the agreed upon limitations that those around you have adopted. You are not limited by inventories, economies, budgets, or any of the other endless list of excuses used by those that have given up on their potential.

You are capable of more than you are doing, otherwise you would not be reading this right now. You have not quit, thus you know you can do more. So quit selling to your quota or limitations and start selling to your potential. The thing that keeps me going is striving to reach my full potential that is inherent in me and has always been there. If you know you can do more, you have an obligation to do more.

Takeaway: Don't accept others expectations.

What GREAT Sales Professionals Must Know

Sales is a monster topic with lots of categories that you must become an expert at. There is no one book or recording that can cover everything you and I need to know in order to become great.

Consider that every salesperson has a unique personality and then add to that that every customer interaction and customer personality is unique and you can see how complicated it can become. Surgery is almost less complicated for the doctor because he is dealing with bodies that are unconscious while the salesperson is dealing with personalities, egos, insecurities, uncertainty, economics, competition and more.

I wish I could be with every person while they are actually in a transaction and then I could be there for you to give you guidance. If you ever come to my offices you will see me jump into the sales department and interact with salespeople to help them close deals. Because I can't be with each of you on every deal, we created a cloud-based technology whereby I deliver solutions to salespeople for every situation.

Takeaway: Sales is more complex than many people realize.

Commit Until Obsessed

Since you have committed to being great at sales and know some of the categories you need to work on, the thing you must do daily is Eat – Drink – Breathe SALES. I don't want you drinking the Kool-Aid. It's time you swim in it and inject it into both arms. You have to become obsessed with this field. I am not kidding here, this needs to become your all-in play. I have never met a great salesperson that didn't see everything he was involved in as a sale. I talk about this in my book Sell or Be Sold. You are either doing the selling or being sold.

The way to become obsessed is to first give yourself permission to become obsessed about something. Then each day when you wake up start with setting your big time goals (check out my 10XPlanner.) Then get some sales training each morning. Then, get some type of motivation on your way to work. Download an mp3 that can sit on your devices so wherever you go you can have positive information being dumped into your space.

I no longer take in any content that can in anyway interfere with where I am going and reaching my potential. This idea of immersion is vital to your commitment to become great. Commit then to being obsessed about doing whatever it takes to become great at what you do. And that requires more than just an idea; it requires the tools, schedule, rituals and follow through.

I start each day by writing my goals, targets, and planning out each minute of the day in my 10X Planner. I get a workout in each morning and then listen to something inspirational while working out and driving to my office. I then hold a sales meeting each morning and role play customer situations with my sales team. On the way home I will duplicate the process in reverse ending the day with another workout and and writing my goals before I go to sleep.

Sales Secret 1
Understanding Rejection

Rejection is that thing responsible for the death of more sales careers and entrepreneurs than probably anything else. How many times has someone said to me, "I can't do sales because I don't like rejection." Every time I hear this from someone I think to myself, just living on planet earth is going to be problematic for that person. Your entire life you have experienced rejections and to be successful at sales or in business or just in life you better get your head wrapped around this topic.

After 30 years of working with salespeople I have come to understand something very important about this topic. Rejection is not what you think it is. Rejection is not an emotion but that thing experienced by those that don't have enough in their pipeline. Rejection is actually an indication that your business model is broken. What I mean is the reason you have this emotional response of disappointment is not because of the obvious outcome or non-outcome in front of you, but the unconscious realization that something about what you are doing is broken.

The fact that the customer says no and doesn't buy is not a reason to be upset, unless of course you don't have any more customers in your pipeline. If the customer says no and there are four more people waiting to buy from you, you may actually find relief and satisfaction that you can move onto those that are able and willing to do business with you. Going forward, I want you to understand that when you experience rejection it is an indication that you have moved away from a scene that is good for you and have become too dependent upon too little.

Takeaway: Rejection isn't what you think it is

The Buyers Insistence 'Tell'

When the buyer adamantly and aggressively insists that they will not do something, it is an indication that they will in fact do that exact thing they suggest they will not. In fact, the more the buyer insists they will not, the more likely they will.

I wish I had a buck for every buyer that has said they would not buy, would not exceed a budget or won't do this or that. When I realized that these were 'tells' of what a prospect would do, I started making sales that had previously escaped me. I remember a prospect once forcibly repeated to me while I was trying to get an appointment to see him, "WE DON'T HAVE THE BUDGET!"

I insisted on getting in front of him as much as he insisted he wouldn't buy and when I finally did get in front of him, not only did he find the budget, he exceeded what I thought he could do.

Think about how many times you scream at your kids, "don't ask me again" and then they do, and you give in. How about the gambler who says "this is my last bet" who then makes another wager. When the buyer takes a strong position in the negotiations and they adamantly repeat themselves about this position, consider this a tell as to some weakness they are experiencing. In poker when the player across from you acts strong they, in fact, may be weak.

I have been involved in very complex negotiations that became extremely emotional when they should not have and I have been on both sides of this phenomenon. I have watched someone get highly enraged saying what they would not do and then doing it and reversing the roles taking a strong position myself, knowing it was nothing more than a negotiating tactic.

TOP SALES SECRETS

Always Always Always Agree

No matter what the buyer says, states or demands, you should under no circumstance, ever disagree or make the buyer wrong or suggest their request is impossible.   This simple strategy is very powerful and will save you lots of sales once you perfect it.

The old saying, the customer is never wrong is not true. In fact, often the customer is wrong; sometimes they even lie, but that doesn't mean you should call them out.   When you tell someone you can't, you won't, you're not allowed to or that's impossible, you only cause this customer to become more dug in on their position and you make it more difficult to come to agreement.

Train, drill and rehearse avoiding all variations of no, not, never, can't and won't. My cloud-based sales university, CardoneUniversity.com actually has built in drills to make sure you get this handled and quit blowing deals. Any and all variations of no and can't must be eliminated from your vocabulary.

Now when you hear this you may think, "I don't want to mislead the customer and I am not going to over promise and then be unable to deliver." The problem here is when you tell someone early on you are unable to do something because you are "so honest'" you just eliminated any chance of being able to do anything for the customer. Try this when a customer asks for the impossible, "I never say no until I have to – if that is possible, there is no better place for you to be."

Role play this law of selling until you no longer get into confrontations with your buyer and make them more difficult than they already are. Perfect "no problem, happy to, my pleasure, exactly what I am thinking, done, you got it" and then learn how to negotiate from a place of agreement. This does not mean that you simply lay down and give the buyer everything they want, It means you use the agreement to keep the negotiations loose enough to be negotiated.

I was recently negotiating a $65 million dollar purchase when the seller said they would not negotiate price under any conditions. I agreed with the seller and suggested that I thought the price was fair and was willing to pay that price based on all the information provided me. I went on to say at any point where I am unable to make sense of the price in our due diligence I commit to you that I will not renegotiate the price. Three weeks into negotiations I called the seller and, true to my word, I told him because of what we found I was going to have to withdraw my offer and because I gave him my word not to renegotiate, I wouldn't. He then asked if they could lower the price for me to close.

Just because this is simple do not underestimate the time and energy necessary to get GREAT at it.

Show A Proposal To Every Customer

Seventy two percent of all salespeople never present a proposal to their customer and eighty seven percent of all salespeople miss their quota. Simply increase the number of people you show a written proposal to and you will close more deals. Interestingly enough, I have found that if a customer is not presented any form of a proposal, it is quite difficult for them to purchase anything... sarcasm intended.

My company is often hired by corporations to help collect data for sales statistics and case studies. Most recently, when consulting for a Fortune 500 company we found that over 70% of all presentations ended with a salesperson greeting the customer, showing the product and then never presenting a financial proposal.

No matter what stage your buyer or prospect is at, you should always present every prospect with a written proposal.

I have worked in industries from appliances to automotive, construction to consulting and real estate to ... and I have yet to see an industry where this didn't apply. Start presenting figures to EVERY prospect, EVERY time, no exception. I don't care what the situation is, present figures. Without a proposal of figures, there can be no close.

Takeaway: Show a proposal.

Show A Proposal To Every Customer

"Excuses for not creating a proposal are not a reason to not present a proposal."

Commonly used excuses for not presenting a proposal:

1. Not ready
2. Not committed
3. Both decision makers not available
4. Still shopping
5. Other opportunities
6. Financing not arranged
7. Inventory not in stock
8. Wasting my time
9. End of my shift

TOP SALES SECRETS

Sales Secret 5
Third Party Touch

Use third parties to improve your position with the buyer and learn things otherwise not uncovered. Put your manager to work on every customer by having the manager or third party touch your customer.

Having another person touch your customer takes the relationship with you and your company to another level. This is often ignored by salespeople that have egos bigger than their paychecks. Using third party touches can turn a prospect into a customer. As a young salesperson in retail, I made it a habit to use a third party to speak to the customer to ensure that I actually had secured the sale or to help assist me in moving the sale to a close. Even when I thought I was successful with a customer and had closed a sale I would get management involved. This involvement with seniors didn't make me look weak, it made me look strong.

This gives a customer service touch, buys a tad more time with the customer, and gives the customer the idea that there is more than just one person in the organization interested in earning their business. A third party touch can be a phone call, an email or a personal visit.

As the owner of the company I still do this when a customer is dealing with our organization whenever possible. At times it is just to thank a prospective customer for the opportunity to work with them and other times it is to close the deal. This speaks volumes to your customers that your organization cares for every client and management is willing to get involved whenever possible to ensure the highest level of customer satisfaction.

Third Party Touch

Use a Third Party to Seal the Deal

Have another party or multiple parties touch every prospect, customer, buyer and non-buyer.

A few situations you can use Third Party Touch

1. Touch early
2. Touch during the presentation
3. Touch in the close
4. Touch on the exit
5. Touch in follow up
6. Secure appointment
7. Email response

Always Provide Options

People love options and you should always provide your buyer with options, even when it appears that your buyer is committed to what you have in front of them! Presenting an option will help them view you in a more consultative role as well as open the door to use inventory / packages /offerings as a way to negotiate instead of using price. When you offer a proposal, make sure you always give the buyer two other options on both sides of the target offer.

One additional option should be something that would include less product or service that may or may not solve the customer's communicated problem. The primary goal of doing this is to help the buyer see more value in the initial proposed solution.

The other additional option should always be a move up or a more expensive or comprehensive alternative to your main proposal. This will likewise either help the prospect see more value in the primary proposal or, better yet, show them that the next level up may be an even more appropriate solution to their problem.

Never present one proposal to a customer NO matter what. The only reason you won't offer options is because you are a scared closer. Trust me, when you can't trust yourself – offer the option.

A = Customer Request

B = Higher

C = Lower

Sales Secret 7
The Second Sale

The Second sale is the most often missed and cost effective opportunity for any company. After consummating the first sale there is a very precise time when the buyer becomes susceptible to another sale. The second sale is the easiest money you will ever make and a tremendous way to increase customer loyalty and repeat business.

Almost 96% of salespeople never attempt a second sale because they are so happy just to make the first one and believe incorrectly that the buyer is out of money. The reality is the buyer almost never gives you or anyone ALL the money they have and will spend more money to support the first purchase. The psychological evidence is everywhere; you see customers making second and third purchases after the first purchase. In many cases the customer went over budget on the first purchase and then continued to go further 'over budget' again and again. The second purchase phenomenon takes place as the customer makes multiple follow up investments to validate the initial purchase decision.

The properly trained sales team with an effective sales process in place can utilize this second sale strategy to increase sales with 15-20% of customers, thereby increasing sales with no increased cost to sell. The opportunity for second sales is strong, as rapport has already been built, the client is already comfortable with you and they trust you as the expert.

The single best way to increase customer loyalty is to cover up your customer in your product and brand. If you believe in your product, your company and in yourself, it stands to reason that the more of your product the customer has, the more they stand to benefit from its use. Now that you understand the opportunity with the second sale it is important to understand how to ask for it. Beware! If not properly executed not only will you not secure the second sale, you also run the risk of losing the initial purchase. So in terms of actually executing the offering of the second sale remember, it's all about timing. When asking for the second sale it is vital to first secure the initial purchase. The first purchase must be done, finished, sold and complete prior to offering the second sale.

If you want to dramatically increase sales volume and deal profitability immediately add the second sale offering to every pitch.

Instant Follow-Up

Consider that forty eight percent of all salespeople never follow up and that 64% of companies admit they do not have any organized way to nurture a lead and you will see follow up is a massive opportunity.

Then add to that the average company takes almost seventy two hours to follow up a lead. Now think with this... by contacting a customer in the first five to ten minutes after the lead is created, your chances of reaching the customer increases 900 times. Text them in the first five minutes and your chances of closing them increases 50X.

Follow Up Magic

- Text Text Text
- Call
- Email
- Mail
- Personal Visit

Takeaway: Learn How to Text and Close

Decision Phenomenon

The buyer decides to take action before he/she agrees to take action, and long before you even get involved with the customer. This is an amazing phenomenon, and once you get your head wrapped around it, it will help you increase your sales. I know veteran salespeople that are unable to wrap their head around this and spend more time selling than necessary. Remember, you don't get paid to sell, talk or present, you get paid to close.

Understand what I am saying - your customer makes a decision to buy and you don't have anything to do with it, except to know when they have made a decision to purchase. The way to do that is ask, "have you seen enough to make a decision?" Or you could tell them prior to the presentation, "if at any point you have seen enough to make a decision just let me know and I will write it up for you."

Consider the possibility that you are actually slowing the customer down from buying when you go on and on presenting. I was recently in a presentation with a buddy of mine who makes upward of $20 million in sales per year. While he was presenting his product to a customer of mine I interrupted him and asked, "have you seen enough to justify the price of John's product?" The customer said no and I told John to continue. John showed another feature and I asked the same question again, "have you seen enough to make a decision?"

Takeaway: Don't present forever, get to closing.

Questions:
Top Sales Secrets

1. What makes the average sales person average, lack of skill or lack of commitment?

2. The way to become obsessed is to first give yourself permission to become _____ about something.

3. What is the thing responsible for the death of more sales careers and entrepreneurs than probably anything else?

4. Having another person _____ your customer takes the relationship with you and your company to another level.

You need to not just sell —you must close

When I realized my life depended on sales and decided to quit moan ing and groaning and made a commitment to being great at sal es, well, everything changed. A guy named Ray told me one day, "You hate sales because you don't know anything about it. Listen to this tape." He gave me a cassette by an old sales trainer who talked about sales like it was a formula for selling step by step from the moment you met the customer to the close. It was amazing. I called the company to asked about what else they had and invested $3000 in a 12 tape training program in 1983. Everyday I invested 30 minut es to one hour watching video footage of this guy explaining sales st ep by step. Within thirty days my production had doubled and, int erestingly enough, what I had been hating on for eight years I now started to enjoy. Within nine months I was in the top 1% in myi ndustry and had fallen in love. Within five years I started a business where I would teach salespeople and sales organizations a new way to sell.

Over the years I have talked to tens of millions of professional sal espeople from every industry. I was speaking to a thousand insura nce agents in Scottsdale, where the average earner in the room made $970,000 a year. I asked them, "How many of you got in to sales because you wanted to be in sales?" Almost no one raised t heir hands. Why don't most people want to be in sales? Because t hey don't know how to close. In order to sell a lot you will have to become a great closer.

Course 6

These days many salespeople spend too much time selling and no time closing. These two are completely different arts. Selling requires you to sell features, benefits and get emotional involvement while the close requires persistence and logic in order to get your customer to make a decision. Closing directs them to take action and exchange money for your product or service. The world is filled with salespeople who never commit to the art of closing the deal

Basics of the Close

You need to have the basics down. This will eliminate fear and discomfort in the close. Only then can you build confidence to handle any prospect.

You'll need to practice with exact scripts and word tracks, correct common mistakes that cost you deals, and practice some more. Closing is the most vital skill in sales, it is where 100% of your income is created. Without the ability to close you will lose.

Basics of the Close

Get Your Head Right

"The close is not for you, it is for the customer."

"The close represents 100% of your earnings."

"The Close is the first time your buyer benefits."

To lock in a sale, you need to have confidence in yourself as well as the product or service you're selling. Closing starts in your head. If you don't have your head right, how will you convince the customer of anything. Lose your confidence and you lose your talent.

Basics of the Close

Words to Never Use in the Close

- No
- I disagree
- Competitive
- Good deal
- We can't do that
- Not possible
- That's our best deal
- No way
- We won't
- WTF

Keep things positive and never make the customer wrong.

Basics of the Close

Requirements for Closing the Sale

- Decision Maker
- Wherewithal
- Sold on the product
- Believe in YOU
- Confidence in the Product
- Written Offer
- Urgency

People want to believe you, but you have to help them. If you have a good product and a good service, then do everything you can to build your case and do it with written information. That way the buyer doesn't have to trust you. Once buyers read that what you're saying is so, they have no choice but to believe you. Make it easy for the buyers to do research while they're with you instead of at home or at their offices when you can't be there.

Basics of the Close

Why YOU Struggle in the Close

- No Commitment to GREATNESS
- Shortage of Closing Material
- Believe Price is the Issue
- Buy the Customer Story
- Unwilling to Pressure
- Lack Financial Goals
- No Training
- Not Sold

Have you ever had a customer tell you that what you're selling costs too much and then goes to your competition only to purchase the same (if not lesser) product at an even higher price? That's proof that the value we know as "price" is a myth. The customer really wasn't talking about the worth of what you're selling but instead, the worth of the sales experience created not being valuable enough for the price. Value comes from the experience that you have built with the customer throughout the sales process.

Price

Always keep in mind that it's almost never price. I guarantee that 9 out of 10 times the issue isn't price. Think back on that last item or service you purchased where you went over budget because you just had that urge. You wanted it so much to the point where you felt like you simply needed it. Price wasn't the factor because you fell in love with that product and were convinced that what you were feeling wasn't a bad thing.

Prove to the client that what they're going to purchase is based off of a decision that will fulfill one of their needs and back it up with incredible service. Once you close that sale, you'll realize that price was a myth all along.

The SECRETS

You're going to have to handle price objections.
Prices are a myth.

- Are you talking to a decision maker?
- Are you talking to someone qualified with the money to buy?
- Do you have a product that people want and will solve their problems?
- Do you want to lower your price or raise your confidence?

Attach Pain to Not Closing

Buyer Benefits from the Close
More than you do

- Buyer gets your product
- Buyer ends shopping cycle
- Problem solved
- Improves Status

Don't get numb to the pain of not closing. If you aren't closing you are losing. *This one skill called "the close" separates those who have, from those who don't have.* Those who do not learn this skill will never have abundance in their life. The close is when a person is able to reap the reward for their previous hard work. *Life is about negotiating.*

Be Sold on the Close

You must attach personal pain to not closing the transaction.

- Lose Confidence
- Lose Security
- Lose Money
- Lose Time
- Lose Momentum
- Start Over again

Respect, credibility and the ability to persist are critical to the close! Your prospect will no longer toy with you when you KNOW how to handle them with confidence and logic. You will become able to control and predict their responses, the results and your income.

All Objections Fall into 4 Categories

- Time
- Money
- Stall
- Product

Christopher Columbus closed the Queen of Spain on funding his travels to the other side of the globe, and then was given credit for the discovery of the New World. Inventor, Ben Franklin, closed the world on electricity and because of him we have light. John Kennedy closed the US population on going to the moon and thus raised the money necessary to fund space travel. If you don't close, it's because of either time, money, a stall, or the product. Closers get by all four objections.

The Urgency Secret

You must build urgency into your close.

The URGENCY must be a legitimate benefit for the Buyer.

No URGENCY = No Close.

- The Urgency Factor is More mental than anything.
- Handle the Why
- Solve a problem
- Provide relief
- Done and over

It is my experience that most people are confused and have the belief that if they know their product, professionally present it while acting enthusiastic, and are nice to the customer, then all will be good. *This is a fantasy.* Get urgent and use urgency.

Set the Stage Close

There are only two reasons you won't make a decision to purchase from me at this time.

1. You aren't the decision maker
2. You can't afford it

Which one is it?

Get to the point. You need to know, so why beat around the bush?

Close the Door on Price

"I don't have any more money
 to give you."

Close the door on money or the customer will
continue to visit it.

You don't want to discount. Keep selling value if price keeps coming up or they
might be on the wrong product.

Pre-Close Intention

My goal is to get your company on our product delivered and installed by _____ (date).

State your intentions early.

Always Get to Price

Never leave a presentation without getting to a price proposal.

How many people never even present a proposal? Too many.

Introduce Price Early

Before I show you the benefit let me share our pricing with you so you can make sense of the value proposition.

This way you can also find out early if you need to move up or down inventory.

The 57% Close

Business buyers are using digital channels to form opinions about major purchases and do not reach out for information until 57% of the purchase process is complete.

- **Do you have enough information to make a decision?**

- **Have you seen enough to make sense of the investment?**

Have Some "Always"

- **Always write a proposal**
- **Always ask to buy**
- **Always ask again**
- **Always introduce 3rd party**
- **Always ask why**
- **Always ask why not**

If you don't have always you'll end up with nevers.

Insistence Required

- **Insistence will be required on 90% of your sales.**
- **Insistence or pressure will never blow a sale.**
- **Without insistence on action now, you will never control your income.**

Instant Trust

How much of what I have said or shared do you believe?

Have you ever noticed when a buyer isn't fully listening to you? This occurs because the prospect assumes that since you are a salesperson they cannot trust you. The media constantly runs broadcasts of scams and cons that make consumers skeptical of salespeople. Losing credibility will add time and this lack of trust from the prospect will cost you sales. Saying "trust me" to a prospect isn't going to build trust and may even have the opposite effect. To properly handle your buyers trust you must understand that people believe what they see, not what they hear. But you can ask them how much of what you have said do they believe.

One Thing Rule

No one thing can blow a sale, ever!

Quit Closing scared.

Remember if you aren't scared you aren't doing anything big. Don't worry about making a mistake, because one thing isn't going to blow the deal.

Reinforce Certainty with Questions

The buyer that is not certain will blame time and money.

- What are you not certain about?
- On a scale from 1-10 how do you feel about the product?
- What other product would solve your problem?
- Is the problem bigger than the investment?

Use Worst Case Scenario

What is the worst thing that could happen if you made a decision?

This is a great question to ask, use it and thank me later.

Get Relevant Event

- **When is the last time your company invested $150,000?**
- **When is the last time you made a decision of this magnitude?**

I have always said if you treat someone like they have money they will act like they have money! Treat me like I won't buy, and I assure you, I will not buy! All of your words, responses, actions, facial expressions, your handling of objections need to communicate that you are treating your prospect as someone who is going to buy, who is going to say yes, who will ultimately go along with your proposal. Treat them like they are going to play and they will play.

Become A Spock Closer

Use emotion to sell the product and use logic to close.

Always smile no matter the outcome, response, objection or communication. This is not just about your internal positive attitude, but also this is regarding your physical manifestation. You have to practice this until you are able to genuinely smile regardless of the situation. The six-month old child does this and melts everyone in her path. Walk around and see how children smile, and you will see the financial value that awaits you by rehabilitating this ability.

SECRETS TO CLOSING THE SALE

Never Return to Selling

Once you enter the close never return to selling.

Most sales people quit because they lack variations of closes. You need a large variety to handle all the various customer types and objections. Remember: correct estimation of effort! It is said that most prospects close after five attempts, but the average salesperson only has four closes available. I don't want four or five, I want hundreds—just in case. Also, you need a complete understanding of your arsenal, not just a familiarity.

**SECRETS
TO CLOSING
THE SALE**

One Question to Reduce Closing Time

- **Why?**
- **Why did you agree to see me?**
- **Why did you come here?**
- **Why did you call here?**
- **Why are you shopping now?**
- **Why?**

Always ask one more time. This is what separates the closers from the sellers, and the big money from the average producer. To continue to ask, persist, to figure out another way to circle back after being told no, reposition the negotiations and ask again is ultimately what will make you a great closer. This requires you have a deep arsenal of techniques and a complete understanding of all the closes in order for you to continue to persist.

Ask One More Time

- **What could I have done differently?**
- **I want to apologize...**
- **Had I done everything right...**
- **What can we do to make this happen?**
- **3rd party close**
- **Exit Survey**

You should always first apologize for not closing a deal as it was your fault, and because of it you weren't able to handle the customer's desire to get something done. Also, always walk your buyer back to where they came from, don't let him leave alone, as this gives you the opportunity to sell him again. Every buyer regrets their decision and second-guesses himself.

Listen But Don't Buy

- **Become completely unreasonable with the buyer's stories, stalls, reasons, & logic.**
- **Stay sold on why it's best for buyer to move forward.**

This area of persistence is also a social issue since you were told as a child that persistence was a bad thing because it was rude and obnoxious. "Can't you listen," "Don't ask me again," and "You are so stubborn" are common negative responses to persistence; however, being stubborn is a good thing. Asking again, and again and again is the sign of someone who knows how to get what they want in life. It is not rude to continue to persist; it is the sign of success and prosperity. Because I continue to ask in another way for a "yes" after being told "no" does not mean I did not listen. It only means I am more sold on my view than I am the other's view.

Treat Objections as Complaints

Treat the objection as a mere complaint until validated as legitimate objection.

Salespeople, unfortunately have been taught to handle objections for years that are not objections at all, but just merely complaints. Of all the sales books I've read, I've never seen this issue distinguished. Over years of research, I learned most so-called objections from the client are not actually objections at all, but just simple complaints that people automatically make throughout life.

Get Something When You Give Something

Never give anything without some reason or without getting something in return.

The winner's exchange is what gives you protection in the marketplace. It is what sets you apart from your competition. The winner's exchange is not about your price but about how people feel when they leave you. The winner's exchange in the close is critical to your success because to the degree the other party really feels like a winner, and leaves excited about being a winner with your product, is the degree to which you can repeat this in the future. Without it you cannot repeat the close.

Zappos, the online shoe company is a great example of winner's exchange. They promise me free shipping for the purchase AND free shipping if I want to return the products. Price has nothing to do with the exchange being a win—the win with Zappo's is removing any risk of loss from the decision.

Check Yourself

- **Do I have the decision maker?**
- **Do they have financial wherewithal?**
- **Are they sold on the product?**
- **Do I know their "Why?"**
- **Will the customer benefit more than price?**
- **Does the customer believe in me?**

It is my experience that most people are confused and have the belief that if they know their product, professionally present it while acting enthusiastic, and are nice to the customer, then all will be good. *This is a fantasy.*

Price Myth

- **No one buys because of price.**
- **You can't buy a price.**
- **A price doesn't make the product better.**
- **Lower Price doesn't increase value.**
- **Price is not a reason to buy or not buy.**

Let's say you live in Calgary and want to take a trip to Phoenix in January to see your family but you find out that you can pay 1/4 of that cost of the Phoenix flight if you go to visit other family in Philadelphia instead. Would you do it? The only way you would reroute your trip to Philly is because you really don't like your family in Phoenix and it would prove to be a winner's exchange for you. You could reason that while going out to Phoenix is more expensive you could make a vacation of it in the desert. You will get honest with yourself that you aren't going to Phoenix in January just to visit your family, you like the idea of the Arizona weather as part of the exchange you receive for visiting your family. Nobody buys on price, it's the value you can reason from it.

Had It Not Been For…

Had it not been for the roofs, landscaping, plumbing issues and estimates on the kitchen our offer would be well within your asking price.

Always show the other party how they are getting what they want.

Wal-Mart has built an entire business model around the lowest price. Do they really offer the lowest price or did Sam Walton just close the world on the idea that it had the lowest price? I suspect it is a little of both. I know that I go there believing they have the lowest price and my reason for going there is that—the lowest price. I don't expect service, I don't expect help, and I know that I will have to put up with long lines.

Agreement Close

Always acknowledge by starting with agreement, then "let me suggest…"

- **"I agree with you"**
- **"You are right"**
- **"100 percent correct"**

Quit turning complaints into objections. You have rich people complaining that it's a lot of money. You have people and companies going over budget and then complaining about their next purchase being too expensive, only to buy all the things they claim are too expensive. If it's a truly valid price objection, then you will use other inventory to move toward.

Second Baseman Close

After validating the 2nd baseman (influencer but not decision maker) ask them:

"Will you be helping with the price, installments or guaranteeing the loan?"

Never neglect other people who may not appear to be involved in the actual deal, but whom, if left out of the conversation, will certainly waste your deal behind your back. Get them involved. The buyer values their opinion more than yours, so use it. Use the second party to assist you in closing the product, or at least find out his considerations, as they will be shared with the buyer and influence his decisions.

Think About it Closes

All "Think about it" closes are really unresolved complaints about:

- **Price**
- **Terms**
- **Product**

"I understand. However, you thinking about it will not change the fact that this product saves you money, your company needs it, and you are going to do it sooner or later. Let's get it done, so you can think about the other things that need attention. I need your approval here and here."

The Unspoken Objection

The most concerning objection is the one you need to hear about.

- **What is your real concern?**
- **What are you not telling me?**
- **If you said everything you were thinking what would you say?**
- **On a scale from 1-10?**

"Great, most people want to take time to think about their decision before making it. Let me ask you, on a scale from one to ten, ten being you are absolutely certain and ready to go, and 1 being you wouldn't take it no matter what, where would you stand at this time?" Get an answer. Then ask, "What would make it a ten?"

Empty Stomach Secret

Never attempt a close when either party is hungry.

There are hundreds of millions of salespeople on this planet who call selling their profession, and they have business cards to prove it. When we talk about successful closers we are talking about a very small, revered club of truly professional, highly trained and highly compensated individuals who have one thing in common—the ability to close, wrap the deal up and tie all the pieces down!

Same Product Close

- **Which product would you rather own if everything else were the same?**
- **Why?**
- **Why else?**
- **Why else?**

This forces a decision regarding with what product the buyer really wants. Find out and handle it. This close will reveal objections you didn't even know were there, which allows you to handle them.

Save Face Secret

- **Never ask "What is your price range?"**
- **Never ask "What is the max you will pay?"**
- **Never ask "What is your budget?"**

More deals are lost over the prospect trying to save face, than are lost over money.

Always Close on a Difference

Never close on the total price. Only make sense of the difference between what is acceptable/expected and what you need.

Buyer has already agreed to some amount/terms. The closer's job is to make sense of the difference.

You must get this next point completely. *If you can't or don't close, then you lose, your family loses, your company loses; and if you believe completely in your product, service, idea or dream, then your customer loses when they don't close on what you represent.* I believe that about the products and services I offer today, and because I believe this with all my heart, I will persist in the negotiation a great deal longer than the average person.

Reduce to Ridiculous Secret

Take the difference amount and divide it by the time of ownership or usage.

$10,000/365 days/8 hours a day

$3.42

"$1000 a month is only $30 a day. You will live in your home, wake up in your home and go to sleep here every day and night. You will build a life here and your family will be safe here for only $30 a day."

Commission Close

Anymore of a discount will result in me NOT getting paid on this transaction and I KNOW you don't want that.

What remains as a profit is my commission and that is the sole way I get compensated and how I take care of my family.

Sign here...

People are more likely to help another human and reduce the need for more of a discount because of the human element than the product itself.

Decision Secret

- **Either way you are going to make a decision.**
- **Not doing it is a decision**
- **Doing it is a decision.**
- **Either way it costs you.**

The buyer has more concern about making the wrong decision than the right one.

"Thought is instantaneous. Think of an elephant. Did you get it? You see, thought is immediate. What you need to do now is make a decision. Yes or no. Do or don't do. I am ok with either one. Which is it?"

Sooner or Later Close

Sooner or later you will make this decision – you need the product, it solves your problems, we are leaders in the field and you can afford it.

Let's do this now so you can start receiving the benefits.

Or the Now or Later close: "Let me suggest that I show you the cost of doing it now and cost of doing it later... The cost now is $300,000. The cost later is approximately 6% more with the new price increases at year-end. That cost equals another $18,000 and a monthly cost of almost $400 that you don't need to waste. Not to mention that with this new product, you, the company, and your clients will benefit without paying the extra cost. Let's do the smart thing. Sign here please."

Persistence and Enthusiasm Close

Please don't confuse my persistence and enthusiasm for earning your business with pressure.

Swiftly respond to this objection with a smile on your face, telling your prospect that he is confusing pressure with enthusiasm. No one resents someone who is confident and excited. You would never blame a child for pressuring a parent because he/she enthusiastically insisted for a yes.

Pressure Response Close

I am willing to pressure you!

The product is right for you and my company is the best solution and waiting doesn't change anything.

Sign here please.

The closer has been taught that pressure and insistence are wrong, ill mannered, rude and inappropriate. Due to his/her upbringing regarding being nice, having manners and other social graces, the salesperson is unwilling to be insistent. While it is important to have manners, and to be respectful to others, this is incorrect data for getting what you want in life.

Reason to Close

Are you looking for reasons to do this or reasons not to?

Be willing to put your decision maker on the spot and close or lose.

This close is to be used when you have a difficult buyer who continues to throw objections at you endlessly with the effort apparently just to be right. Be careful with this one. Once you get the buyer to agree that he is looking for reasons to do it, then ask him for those reasons and put attention on the positives, not the negatives. Use this late in the negotiations.

Copy or Paperwork Close

I am happy to get you as many copies as you would like. Give me one minute.

As I was making the copies of the proposals...

Mr. Buyer, I realized when I was making a copy for you, that if this product was exactly what you wanted and the figures were exactly right, I wouldn't be making a copy, I would be getting you a delivery and installation date instead. What is not right?"

Perfect Close

If everything were perfect would you still continue to wait? What's not perfect?

"There is never a perfect time to make this decision as you will always have things going on. Let's do this now and get it handled for you so you can start benefiting now. Sign here and here please."

No Other Objections

If there are no other objections, questions or reasons not to move forward I will need your approval here and here...

Flush out all stalls and close.

This shows understanding and acknowledges the person for wanting to make a good decision. This helps flush out hidden objections as to why this might not be the best decision for them.

Questions:
Secrets to Closing the Sale

1. What is the most vital skill in sales?

2. The close isn't for you, it's for the _____?

3. Make a list of words to never use in the close:

4. Are prices a myth? Yes / No

5. This one skill called _____ separates those who have, from those who do not.

6. Introduce price: early, in the middle of the pitch, or at the end?

7. No one thing can blow a sale, ever! True / False

When You Fail to Close —Follow Up

In the confrontation between the stream and the rock, the stream always wins; not through strength, but through perseverance. – Buddha

I cannot overemphasize how important follow up is for you to make the number of sales it's going to take to get super rich. If you get great at one thing, get great at follow up.   It's the greatest sales secret of all-time. The money is in the follow up. Consider that 48% of all salespeople never follow up and 64% of companies admit they do not have any organized way to nurture a lead. This is a game changer and a way to dominate your market if you follow up better than the competition. Keep in mind the average company takes almost 72-hours to follow-up a lead and you can see why contacting a customer in the first 5 to 10 minutes increases your chances of closing the customer 900 times!

Course 7

Don't feel bad if you aren't doing a great job of follow up. The reality is none of us were taught creative ways to follow up. Beyond a manager just saying, "follow up" over and over—there has been very little instruction on the topic. Some companies have surrendered to the idea that their people will not follow up and pay other companies to send cookies and mail.

Follow Up:
THE GREATEST SALES SECRET OF ALL TIME

FOLLOW-UP
THE GREATEST
BUSINESS SECRET

"The great salespeople aren't talkers they're professional stalkers."

FOLLOW-UP
THE GREATEST
BUSINESS SECRET

DAY ZERO – 5 MINUTE FOLLOW-UP

"Thanks for your time – Call me 310-777-0255."
Thank you Text within the first 5 minutes of contact.

You increase conversion by 9x by following up within 5 minutes.

SAME DAY - FIRST CALL BACK

Within the hour of contact

"Thank you for the opportunity it was a pleasure working with you..."

- Any Questions?
- What did I miss?
- If everything was perfect?
- On a scale from one to ten?
- Who else would be involved in the process?

"I'm in a hurry to help and I act like it." – GC

DAY 1 – THE 24 HOUR CONTACT

"I have a great idea and would like to set up a time to meet either in person or over video conference call."

Or

"I have a great idea give me a call back."

(text, email or VM)

"Time is money – act like it." – GC

FOLLOW-UP
THE GREATEST
BUSINESS SECRET

DAY 2 – 48 HOURS

Write handwritten letter
followed up by text and email

"Dear,

Thanks for connecting.
I have some information I want to send you
concerning our recent conversation."

"More important people than you take time for handwritten notes." -GC

DAY 2 – 48 HOURS

Text / Email / Call / VM

"Want to be sure I have the right address I have something special to send you. Text me back at..."

"I will make more phone calls in first 24 hours to one prospect than 95% of all salespeople." –GC

DAY 3

Text / Email / Call / VM

"Hey John, I wanted to put a face to the name.

Give me a call back – 310-777-0255.

My management team and I met and we have some great ideas to earn your business."

"Put a face to your service and you become more real to your prospect."– GC

DAY 4

Personal Visit

"John I want to fly out and meet with you and your team."

"Take time out of the sale by removing distance from of the sale."– GC

DAY 4

Thought of You Follow-Up

"I was thinking of you and saw your new commercial – congrats great job. By the way, can you call me back with who your creative is..."

"I think of the unsold everyday."– GC

DAY 10

Event Offer

"We have a great event coming up and wanted to invite you and your business to attend."

"If you can't sell your friends and your family you need to have your head examined." – GC

DAY 14

Informational Links

"Noticed the movement in the 10 year today and thought of you. Call me if I can help – 310-777-0255."

http://data.cnbc.com/quotes/US10Y

"The use of 3rd party data can make anyone look like a genius." – GC

Organic Plan Creative

Day 21 - Video Email

Day 30 - Event Offer

Day 40 - Thinking About You

Day 50 - Special Offer

Day 60 - Personal Visit Offer

Day 75 - Photo Mockup

Day 90 – Management Call

Day 100 - Special Gift

Day 120 - Personal Visit

Day 150 - Drop off special offer

Day 180 - Compelling Information

Day 210 - Just got this in via text

Day 240 - Apology Contact

Day 270 – Chocolate boot

Day 300 - Personal of Influence

Day 330 - Testimonial Request

Day 365 - Anniversary Close Call

"IN THE CONFRONTATION BETWEEN THE STREAM AND THE ROCK, THE STREAM ALWAYS WINS; NOT THROUGH STRENGTH, BUT THROUGH PERSEVERANCE."

– Buddha

FOLLOW-UP
THE GREATEST
BUSINESS SECRET

FOLLOW-UP FACTS

FOLLOW-UP
THE GREATEST
BUSINESS SECRET

The Importance of Follow-Up

- 2% of all sales made on the 1st contact
- 3% of all sales made on the 2nd
- 5% of all sales made on the 3rd
- 10% of all sales are made on the 4th
- 80% of all sales made between 5th-12th

Not Organized

Lazy

False Expectations

Bad Information

Too Many Leads

Undefined

No Plan

Why Do So Many
Fail at Follow-Up?

Lack of Motivation

Management

Not Required

Ethics

No Accountability

Being Reasonable

Social Training

No Commitment

FOLLOW-UP
THE GREATEST
BUSINESS SECRET

Follow-Up Defined

Something that continues or completes a process or activity.

SEE SOMETHING ALL THE WAY THROUGH.

The Reality of Lead Conversion

- 73% of B2B leads not "sales ready"

- 50% of "qualified leads" not ready

FOLLOW-UP
THE GREATEST
BUSINESS SECRET

Grant Cardone
Follow-Up Reality

100% Of All Leads Convert

Why You Need To Nurture Leads?

1. Because no one else does
2. It's the right thing to do
3. You will slip into obscurity if you don't

FOLLOW-UP
THE GREATEST
BUSINESS SECRET

COLLAPSE TIME

Follow up in the first 60 seconds and you will have an almost 500% increase in conversion.

BE FIRST

- 1st to follow up has 248% greater chance of converting vs. the 2nd or 3rd

- 37% of businesses respond in the first hour

- 7x more likely to have a meaningful conversation with Decision Maker if contacted within the 1st hour

The "ALWAYS" Rule

ALWAYS use multiple forms of communication

Forms of communication

- Phone
- Text
- Voicemail
- Email
- Video
- Links
- Personal Visit
- Social
- Gifts

FOLLOW-UP
THE GREATEST
BUSINESS SECRET

WHY PEOPLE DON'T BUY FROM YOU

FOLLOW-UP
THE GREATEST
BUSINESS SECRET

You Have To Understand
The "WHY"
To Understand
The "HOW"

In most cases it has nothing to do with you

"People don't buy from people they like, they buy from the people in front of them when they are ready to buy." – GC

- **Lack of Time**
- **Personal Issues**
- **Concerns About Cost**
- **Change of Guard**
- **Not the Decision Maker**
- **Wrong Product**
- **Not Ready To Buy**

FOLLOW-UP
THE GREATEST
BUSINESS SECRET

"YOU ARE RESPONSIBLE REGARDLESS OF THE REASON."

– Grant Cardone

FOLLOW-UP MISTAKES

FOLLOW-UP
THE GREATEST
BUSINESS SECRET

Pick Up the Phone B*%$#

MAKE THE CALL

48% of all salespeople don't make the call

Most companies fail with follow-up because they simply lack the creativity necessary to stand out and get a customers attention. If you say the same thing every time you follow-up, it is only a matter a time before the salesperson is sick of repeating themselves and the customer is sick of getting the call.

Frequency leads to Greatness

Five to twelve calls, not one or two, is what you need to think with for follow-up.

"What I lack in intelligence I make up with persistence." – GC

Without commitment, nothing else matters. Sadly, this is where most companies fail before they even get started, they simply have not even made a commitment to follow-up. In fact, 48% of organizations never even make the 1st follow-up attempt.

Get Regular

Be consistent and regular...
be there all the time.

"With follow up, be the stream, not the rock." – GC

Get Organized – Use a CRM to log ALL client interactions and the context of every contact so that you can strategically follow-up with your prospect without repeating information covered in a previous contact.

Waiting Too Long To Follow-Up

The odds of contacting a lead decrease 10X in the 1st hour.

"Waiting too long... Don't do it to yourself, your customer or your business." – GC

Speed - I always say time kills all deals. But it definitely kills contact rates. You are 9x more likely to convert a prospect if you respond within 5 minutes. After 60 minutes, that number drops 100X.

Lack of Variety of Reasons to Call

Because you lack variety you become predictable and run out of reasons to follow up.

Use everything in your arsenal.

"The broken record follow-up strategy will always fail you." – GC

No Clear Purpose in the Call

Calling without a reason will become an annoyance and a waste of your prospect's time.

"If you don't have a reason to call... your customer won't have a reason to talk to you." – GC

Not Leaving a Message

Whether you're on the phone, leaving a message in person, or emailing NEVER make them feel bad, just leave a message!

"Always, always, always leave a message." – GC

Not Collecting Critical Data – For Future Sales

Not collecting critical data for future sales is ridiculous. Whether you sell cars, watches, furniture, or investment portfolios, you need critical data for future sales. Consumers try and reinforce the first purchase by thinking about a second purchase. Have you ever been in the furniture store and bought something and then on the way home think to yourself how you should have gotten that side table in addition to what you already purchased? It happens to everyone. Always look for other potential sales, buying cycles, and what's next.

FOLLOW-UP
THE GREATEST
BUSINESS SECRET

Not Asking For Referrals

There is no rule, just know this:

Ask, Ask Often, Ask Frequently, and KEEP ASKING.

- **DON'T SAY:** "If you know anybody, send them my way."
- **DO SAY:** "Who do you know that would benefit from my product or service?"

"Almost every customer will give you referrals and almost every salesperson fails to ask for them." – GC

No Clear Purpose

If a person is going to call, there must be a reason. You need a reason. The way I start my calls is "The reason I'm calling is..." I tell everyone the reason upfront. If your purpose is to ask about the kids, the wife, the vacation—then let that be your purpose and don't sell the product. Just make it clear. Be honest about your purpose and you'll always have one. If you have a clear purpose going into a phone call you have no excuse to not make it.

Not leaving a message is something that should never be done but more salespeople do this than don't. You don't want to seem desperate? Why not? You are desperate. Who are you kidding? Are you hungry for business? Then let people know it. I don't know why people worry about the idea of "appearing" desperate. Every time I call someone, I'll leave a message. Never make them feel bad for not calling you back, stay friendly, and just leave a message.

Phone Calls are one of my most preferred ways to follow up. I go through all the same doubts that you do—am I being too persistent? will they answer? will they tell me not to call anymore? or will they deny me? I go through all that—but at least I know I'm talking to someone. If I talk to enough people, I'll sell something. Where do you call? Call cell first, then office, then home. Who do you call? Everybody.

When I make a call, I actually make 6 or 8 phone calls. When I call a company and ask for Bob and Bob's not there, I ask for his voicemail. I leave a message and then call the receptionist again and ask who is underneath Bob. She says it's Jack, then I ask for Jack and get his voicemail. "Hey Jack I just left a voicemail with Bob and wanted to leave a voicemail with you, here is my number." Then I go back to the receptionist and ask for who is under Jack. Shelly is. I call her and she finally picks up. It's the first contact of the day. You see, I don't just leave messages, I always talk to somebody. Remember to always have a specific reason for calling. Start with "The reason I'm calling is…". Also keep it tight—people don't have all day.

FOLLOW-UP
THE GREATEST
BUSINESS SECRET

Phone Call

- Add Value – Have a Reason for Call
- Pay attention
- Have a good attitude
- Don't make them feel obligated
- Quickly make the call
- Be friendly, have a positive attitude

Mistake: **No Phone Call**—Why would a salesperson not follow-up even once on a potential client? Not even one little phone call! Those that never make the call will come up with lots of excuses as to why they don't. They're too busy organizing, searching the CRM, thinking about what they're going to say, looking for a script. People come up with reasons not to make a call. You need to be unreasonable and make the call regardless of any reason you come up with not to.

Text

This is the number one preferred way to follow up. It's preferred because it's so easy and so fast. If you're going to have one contact, the cell phone is it. It's not their home phone and it's not their e-mail. Make it a priority to ask, "what's your cell number?" or even a better way, "where can I text this to you?" It can be a piece of information, a photo—just ask where you could text the data to. Another move is to just ask to take a picture of them with the product and then send it.

I've never had a customer deny my request to take a photo of me and them on their phone that I could text back to myself. Try texting data during the sale. When someone is requesting data from you, if you text them during the sale the chance of converting them goes up 300%. The cell phone has proven to be the number one tool when following up a potential customer. Make it a priority— your primary focus should be on the text.

FOLLOW-UP
THE GREATEST
BUSINESS SECRET

Email

This is one of my least preferred ways of follow up but it's still necessary. It's a lazy follow up but because everyone has an email address, it's necessary. People think they follow up because they sent an email. Look, if the email didn't get to them, you didn't send it. Remember that saying about when a tree falls in the forest and nobody is there did it make a sound? If you send an email and it goes to spam, nothing happened. Nobody heard anything, the message wasn't completed, there is no communication, and therefore there is no follow up. I hate emails. You know why? Because I don't know for sure if they got them which means I'm left in doubt. The reason I follow up is so I can come out of doubt.

Emails are also forgotten very quickly. They get lost. Today I got maybe 60. Who texts me? My friends do. People that are close to me. Who emails me? Everybody. That's why in an email you need to embed a call to action and a phone number. That number should be your cell not your office number. This is a huge mistake many people make. People don't make a call to action, the text is too long, no promises, no big claims, and there is never a cell phone. Know email is weak, it's lazy, but you've got to use it.

Handwritten Letter

- Lost art
- Opportunity to differentiate yourself
- You can dominate in this area
- Takes time, but it's EXTREMELY personal

This is a great way to add personal touch.

FOLLOW-UP
THE GREATEST
BUSINESS SECRET

Personal Visit

- This is the most powerful follow-up
- Takes time out of the equation
- Easy to hang up a phone, hard to kick someone out of office

  - 63% of companies don't follow-up.
  - Do what others refuse to do.

Technology seems to be moving at super-sonic speed. And while it may appear to be revolutionizing the way business is done with emails, text messages, Facebook, Twitter, and other applications, none of these tools can or will ever replace the VALUE provided by the personal touch. Your customer craves the personal influence of a professional, positive human being that becomes the face of your company and your product! Do NOT be deceived by the technology drive! As it becomes bigger and more prevalent the need for human interaction, the personal touch, becomes even more desirable and more valuable. An email or a text is nothing compared to a personal visit!

Using Gimmicks

- Gimmicks Get attention
  – break through the noise.
- Communicate personality
  through your follow-up.

It's so important to stand out in this competitive marketplace. Seek to be memorable! Now, I'm not talking about using gimmicks or tricks. I mean get creative. Be unique by your actions and let what you do set you apart and put you on track for success. When you seek out new ways to impress and service customers and clients, it really challenges you and inspires creativity. You'll be motivated to look for ways to provide that WOW factor and smash the competition. Far too often people coast along on average by doing the minimum. Why not deliver a wow experience for clients and customers by being creative in your actions?

FOLLOW-UP
THE GREATEST
BUSINESS SECRET

Apology Contact

- What did we do wrong?
- Where did I miss it?
- Can I get some feedback?
- What could we have done differently?

FOLLOW-UP
THE GREATEST
BUSINESS SECRET

Cell Phone Video Message (Selfie)

- Selfie Benefits: Low production, high volume, inexpensive, tremendous separation from others

- The average person reads 1 book/year but watches 750 videos/year.

- Keep it SHORT: 30 seconds

FOLLOW-UP
THE GREATEST
BUSINESS SECRET

Social Media Reach

Facebook, Google+, Twitter, LinkedIn, YouTube, Snapchat, Periscope, Blab, Meerkat

Social media isn't just about getting known, it's about you being able to get to know your clients and follow up on them.

Newsletters and Blogs

Content is King.

Having content gives you something to promote.

It's a way to communicate about your ideas, company, industry or product.

FOLLOW-UP
THE GREATEST
BUSINESS SECRET

Use Photo Images

People process images 60,000 times faster than words.

Technology allows for creative images or pictures to be sent easily.

Testimonials

- Testimonials as follow-up reinforce successes others have had with your product or service.

- Gives a creative reason to follow-up

- With the unsold – allows them to sell themselves on your company

FOLLOW-UP
THE GREATEST
BUSINESS SECRET

Survey

Exit Survey

- Did our solution solve your problem?
- Did we get you a proposal on it?
- Were we within your budget?
- On a scale of 1-10, how would you rate our solution that we provided you?
- What is your biggest concern at this time?
- What would we have to do to earn your business at this time?

"BE SO PERSISTENT YOU STAND OUT AS THE ONLY CHOICE."

– Grant Cardone

FOLLOW-UP
THE GREATEST
BUSINESS SECRET

Questions: Follow-Up

1. Increase your conversion _____ by following up within 5 minutes.

2. What is the day 50 Follow-Up?

3. Why do so many fail at Follow-Up?

4. Are phone calls one of the most preferred ways to follow up?

5. What is Grant Cardone's least favorite way to follow up?

Great Follow-Up to a Great Life

Once you get great at sales, great at closing, great at follow up, you've got your personal finances right and are on your way to millions, you are ready for the 10X Super Life. This isn't just about finances, although finances are an important area of your life. You don't just want to be a millionaire, you want to have abundance in EVERY area of your life. What good does a million dollars do you if your health sucks? I want it all. I want you to have it all.

Course 8

The majority of people live an average life, following the status quo, and only making 'realistic' goals. Have you ever wondered what it would be like to live a Super Life? You wouldn't be the first. A Super Life has been achieved by many, but what is a Super Life to you? For me a Super Life is having a super family, having a super reputation in my industry, running super businesses, having super physical health, super money, super wealth and super spiritual purpose. To live a Super Life I would have abundance in all of these areas of my life—not seeking balance or average. I spent the first 40 years of my life thinking too small, being too careful and too conservative in my actions—in both my personal and professional life. I don't want you to take that same path. I want you to begin creating your Super Life now so you can get as massive as you can.

MY MISSION

"To build a viable network of like-minded people committed to creating extraordinary Super Life Success in every aspect of their lives."

I want to meet seven billion people. Whether it's a single mom with two kids or whether it's a guy coming back from Afghanistan starting over, or whether it's a guy 51 years old, redefining where his career is, you can meet people that are moving toward the Super Life.

10X SUPER LIFE

"PEOPLE ARE SETTLING FOR THEIR REALITY RATHER THAN WORKING TO THEIR FULL POTENTIAL."

– Grant Cardone

10X SUPER LIFE

Super Defined

- Above or beyond
- To a great extreme
- Extra large
- Having greater influence, capacity
- Of a higher kind

Origin – above, beyond

What is super? Have you even looked up the word super? Or do you just think Superman when I say Super? You're like, OK, well, Superman's not real but the word super is real. If you define the word, it's above or beyond. To a great extreme, extra large, having greater influence or capacity of a higher kind.

Takeaway: To be super you have to know what it means.

10X Defined

"The right think, combined with the right amount of actions across all of your life's interests, to accomplish an extraordinary life; referred to as Super Life."

"Trade in your ideas of settling for I want it all." -GC

Extraordinary Defined

- Very unusual or remarkable

Origin – Outside the normal course of events

Extraordinary defined is very unusual or remarkable. Were any of your classes in high school about becoming unusual or remarkable? "Hey, you guys, we're going to remarkable class." This was not taught to you, it was not encouraged, it was actually beaten out of you. Some of you had it spanked out of you, hammered out of you, or verbalized out of you.

Takeaway: You've been taught not to be extraordinary.

Freedom Defined

- The power or right to act, speak or think as one wants without hindrance or restraint
- State of being able to move freely
- Using or expending something without restraint

Origin

Free – not in bondage, to love, think of lovingly

Dom – master (control or authority)

Takeaway: There's much more to freedom than just finances.

Success Defined

- The accomplishment of an aim or purpose
- The attainment of popularity or profit
- Person that achieves desired aims or prosperity

Origin – come after, to follow

Success doesn't mean you're rich. Look at the definitions. If you don't have a dictionary in your office, remember one of the traps is not understanding something. If I don't know something, I'm not dumb. Maybe there's a lie. Maybe there's a lack of knowledge. Maybe I never looked up the word. I know I went to 17 years of school, got a good degree in accounting, and never looked at the single word success, and the only reason I went to college was to accumulate success.

Takeaway: Success is not just about finances.

Success expansion is vital across all your interests to **Survive.**

You must become something you commit to. You do not want to be successful in one area, you want to be greedy and be successful in every area of life.

Survive Defined

- Continue to live or exist in spite of danger or hardship.

When I understood this word, literally, it changed my entire life. Survive, to continue to live or exist in spite of danger or hardship. I thought it meant to barely get by. That's what I thought. The first 37 years of my life was just..."surviving". It didn't matter how much I had, I was broke. I was just getting by. I had five million dollars in a bank account. And every day I'm terrified. Every day I'm scared. Continue to live or exist in spite of danger or hardship. That means your marriage would live on despite danger or hardship.

Takeaway: Learn the true meaning of survive

Survive Defined

- Remain alive after death.
- Super Live
- Above, Beyond Life

Here's another definition of it, to remain alive after death. I become very fascinated with this. This is interesting content for me, only because I've always been extremely inquisitive about the spiritual nature of things. And when everybody told me "you can't know that," I even got more interested because any time somebody says you can't know, I say, "Oh, man, there must be some gold behind that door."

Takeaway: Survive applies to more than just finances.

Failure Defined

Failure is everywhere folks. A falling short, a deficiency. Any time you have a deficiency, a falling short in love, time, money, resources, wealth, decisions, choices—you are failing. You must share this with everyone in your company and your family. If you get on the phone, you make a pitch, you don't get an order, you failed. I don't care what the excuse is. " He's not in. He's not the decision maker. The price is too high, it's ridiculous." You failed. It is what it is.

Be honest with your people. It is failing. you set a target right here. You didn't hit it. You failed. Falling short, a deficiency. You don't have money in the bank to survive three months, six months, ninety months. That is your failing. It's not bankruptcy. It's called failing. It's called a deficiency.

Takeaway: Failure is everywhere, own up to it.

Origin of the word Failure:

The origin of the word failing seven hundred years ago, probably fourteen hundred years ago, was to lose strength or weaken, fade away or die. Let's keep it real, man. "Oh man, I'm failing." No, you're dying. You're fading away. To be unsuccessful is the word failure. If you're failing, you're unsuccessful until you get honest. You've got a drinking problem. The moment you say, "I've got a problem," you can fix that problem. The moment you realize the tire is flat, the transmission is broken, you can fix it. But if you're denying it, you can look up the word failing all the way back to what it originally meant because you know, back in the day, 700, 800, 900 years ago, it was crude. They told you the truth.

Now we say you are right. You went to class, you graduated. You finished last, here's a consolation prize. Could I fail physically and be bankrupt physically? How many of you know people that are physically bankrupt and they have physically bankrupted their body? People say, "Man, where do you get your energy from?" I create it. "Man, I'm so tired all the time." That's because you're bankrupt physically. You are failing. You're deficient. You're dying, don't you understand? Death doesn't happen when it happens. It's been happening, man. It's been happening. You don't die on a certain date. My mom died on a certain date, right? She didn't die that day, it had been happening for a while. We all just denied it.

Takeaway: Get real with failure.

Live by this FACT

"I know people that are dead at 25 and don't make it official until they're 80." - GC

False knowledge, no knowledge, and a false sense of security are only accepted by those that have not committed to **CREATE** a super extraordinary 10X LIFE of freedom.

Takeaway: If you don't start living you'll start dying.

When you are unable to survive you are unable to continue into the future beyond technological disruptions, economic contractions, and unplanned events.

Get it all. If you don't get it, if you waste it, you lose. It's not greed, it's wanting a Super Life. Every person should have this desire.

Takeaway: Get it all, have a Super Life or you won't survive.

Extra Defined

- An item that in addition to what is usual or strictly necessary

Origin – shortening of extraordinary

When I turn to Superman we're not talking Marvel comic books, we're talking about abundance and prosperity. And if you don't have it, there's something you don't know. We're talking about success. Success doesn't happen to you. If it does, you're in trouble. Success happens because of you, nothing happens to you. It happens because of you.

Takeaway: Go beyond the normal.

"The pursuit and attainment of my full potential across ALL of my life and what I produce lives on beyond me." -GC

Motivation is a monster problem for most people. What motivates you? How do you stay motivated? How do you stay energized and creative? This is a challenge for everyone, even the motivational speakers. Having energy, being happy, being motivated to meet new people and expand your network takes energy and most importantly it takes a sense of excitement about your future. Think BEYOND you.

Takeaway: What you produce will live on.

Life Defined

- Particular type or aspect of people's existence
- Vitality, vigor or energy
- Period between birth and death

Origin – to live

Are you truly alive or are you just slowly dying? To live you must show up. The number one rule in creating success is to show up, to merely just show up. In fact, it's been said that 90% of all success people encounter is about showing up.

 Just show up folks. Ever known someone who got lucky a lot? You know what they did? They showed up. You can't get lucky if you don't show up, so suit up and show up. All highly successful people know they have to show up—and that's what they do. They just keep showing up.

Takeaway: Life starts with showing up.

Why You Don't Have a Super Life

- **Wrong role models**
- **Wrong definitions**
- **Wrong targets**
- **Education**
- **Lack of revenue**

Takeaway: A common theme of those who don't have a Super Life is "small".

Role Models

Parents, teachers, peers & media promote average as the safe haven when it is not.

"The average level of action is the most dangerous, because it is accepted by society as enough." - The 10X Rule

Do you know why airlines tell you to put the mask on yourself before you try to assist others? Because it's an inevitable truth, that unless you take care of yourself first, you will never be able to take care of others. How can others help you when they can't help themselves? You've been taught by people who are drowning financially.

Takeaway: You've had the wrong role models teaching you average is okay.

Lies of Society

- **Don't stand out**
- **Be seen and not heard**
- **Don't ask me again**
- **You aren't special**
- **Seek balance**
- **It's the journey not the destination**
- **Be satisfied with what you have**
- **High expectations lead to disappointment**
- **Set reasonable goals**
- **Takes money to make money**
- **Successful people are unhappy**
- **Be grateful you have more than most**
- **You can't have it all**
- **You have to balance life and work**
- **Under promise and over deliver**

Which of these have you bought into?

Takeaway: Society teaches you many wrong ideas from a young age. You must shed these.

"MOST OF US ARE BROUGHT UP POOR AND MIDDLE CLASS. THEN BARELY LIVE THE REST OF OUR LIVES, STUCK WITH THE BELIEFS OF THE POOR AND THE MIDDLE CLASS."

– Grant Cardone

Middle Class Goals Conflict with Freedom

- **Buy a Home**
- **Job Security**
- **Conveyer Belt Education**
- **Income Focus**
- **Play it Safe**

I was recently asked, *"What is your biggest fear?"*

Without hesitation I said, *"Not being able to make a difference in the lives of enough people."* For me, this super spiritual purpose would allow me to make a massive difference for the better of the entire planet! Your conflict with freedom is that nobody knows you. The more attention you get the more money you can make. Money follows attention. This is at odds with the above middle class goals.

Takeaway: Get attention, not a home and job security.

10X SUPER LIFE

False Knowledge

- **Family is everything**
- **There is a shortage of money**
- **I don't have time to work out**
- **Follow your feelings**
- **I can't know the truth**
- **Life is short**
- **I can't have it all**
- **Most marriages fail**
- **Not everyone can make it**
- **You have to have reasonable goals**

Almost any common "saying" that the general public believes to be true is false if you analyze it closely.

Takeaway: Don't just accept as true the "proverbs" people tell you.

Can you Survive Danger & Hardship?

Can you survive the condition you're in right now? Bad things are going to happen to you, folks. I guarantee you. You're going to have a daughter that ends up with some kind of health care issue. She doesn't have any money, she doesn't have a job and mom has got to pay the bill, and it's not going to be covered. Mom, is going to be like, "Oh, this treatment will be covered but I don't want to do that. So I do this other thing that's not covered." Bam, $36,000. Wasn't in the budget, wasn't in the plans, nobody would ever come up with a list of everything that is going to happen to you in this thing called life. See, your mommy and daddy just thought it was a bad break. The government tells you this.

People go bankrupt. They say the number one reason people go bankrupt is because of health problems. No, they don't. They don't go broke because of health problems. They didn't have enough resources in the bank to cover the unexpected $300,000 brain cancer surgery.

Takeaway: Bad things happen in life, you need enough money to take care of them.

Universal Fact

The middle class will not survive hardship and danger. You're not in a position to weather the storm. Look back to 2008, look at all the people that lost everything... I mean your home is supposed to be your safe haven. How many thousands and thousands and thousands of people lost their homes, right? Wrong math. Wrong because the economy crashed because they weren't in a financial situation deal with it. Universal facts. Bad things happen to good people. Bad things happen to extraordinary people. Only one group survives.

There's only two groups that's all there is. There are not three groups. Quit thinking you're in the middle. There are two groups, those that will survive and those that will not. Survive means to go on into the future. Here's the major difference. The group that will survive is committed to freedom.

Takeaway: Survive means to go into the future.

Major Differences

The group that will survive is willing to invest resources. The group that will survive is willing to use debt. Dave Ramsey says you shouldn't even borrow money to have a car to produce a job. He basically said "Hey, you can't be free with that." And you also can't be free because you won't use debt. You might need to use debt to get your freedom. Why would I not want to sign a piece of paper to put myself in a better position? It's just power, right?

Commit to freedom and be willing to invest resources. The first group that will survive invests time to know how to do something. They win because they are obsessed with freedom. I'm not talking about money, and I'm not talking about wealth. I'm talking about the biggest compliment you will ever be given in your life—freedom.

Takeaway: One group of people are committed to freedom, one group isn't.

WARNING

The two wealthiest people I know both said this, "You're the freest guy I know." I'm like, "I wish I had your paper." "Bro, you're the freest dude I know." I said, "What does that mean?" "That you do what you want. You dress how you want, you go where you want, you say what you want. I mean, you tell jokes that other people like." It's not just the money, man. I don't want a billion dollars if if it means I can't speak my truth. I don't want two billion dollars or five billion dollars or fifty billion dollars if I can't come and go as I please and do what I want. I don't want to go public with Wall Street. If they're going to be banging on me and saying, "Hey, we own you."

Run for your life from all ideas that trap you into an existence that is anything close to merely normal. Run for your life. This needs to be your decision. Our goal is to create a super extraordinary life. You must first change your think. The first thing you have to do is change this. You literally have to go in and absolve yourself of any thinking that traps you and replace that with new data.

Takeaway: Run from anything that is normal.

"TO CREATE A SUPER EXTRAORDINARY 10X LIFE FOR YOURSELF & OTHERS YOU MUST CHANGE YOUR THINK. THIS STARTS WITH ABSOLVING YOURSELF OF THE THINKING THAT TRAPS YOU AND REPLACING THAT WITH NEW INFORMATION."

– Grant Cardone

10X SUPER LIFE

"I AM COMMITTED TO CREATING MY SUPER EXTRAORDINARY LIFE OF FREEDOM AND SUCCESS."

– Grant Cardone

10X SUPER LIFE

"High expectations are the key to everything."
- Sam Walton

Sam Walton created one of the biggest organizations in the world. He is among the U.S. Army, the Indian army, the Chinese army, as the biggest employers in the world. High expectations. "High expectations are the key to everything." Sam Walton, founder and creator of a Wal-Mart. He's from Bentonville. There's more people working at one Wal-Mart than all the people that lived in Bentonville when he lived there.

Takeaway: Have high expectations.

EXCUSES WHY YOU DON'T HAVE IT ALL:

- Job
- Money
- Marriage
- Single
- Bad breaks
- Physical condition
- Government
- Upbringing
- Kids
- Boss
- Location

Takeaway: Excuses are everywhere. No, you failed and came up short.

10X SUPER LIFE

EXCUSES

I had a guy in here the other day with one leg, and the left one didn't work. Right one's going, left one didn't work. I said, "How's the left one?" "Better than the right one." He's joking about it. Had another guy in here the other day, got one eye. I said, "Hey, which eye do I look at?" He started laughing, he said, "Nobody ever asked." I said, "I got to know, is it the left one or the right one? Which one do I look at?" He said, "Look at the right one, that's the one that works."

Freedom, baby. freedom to say whatever you want, when you want, how you want. Right? Freedom, man. What's going to happen to me by me saying, "David, David. Which eye, bro?" What's going to happen to me? Nothing's going to happen to me. We actually are in a better relationship because I finally got this thing like, I don't know, man, which one?

Government is causing you so much harm, of course. Daddy ignored you. Or Daddy paid you too much attention. The uncle that ignored you, the uncle that touched you. Your upbringing, your kids, your boss, your location. How many other reasons? What else we got? How many other excuses? There's a lot of them. What excuses are you making that are preventing you from living the 10X Super Life?

Takeaway: You can't have a 10X Super Life making excuses.

Aspects of YOUR Life

- Family
- Business
- Health
- Spiritual
- Financial
- Community
- Recreation

You can have a great life in 5 areas but have hardship in two. You can just have one great area and the other six fail. The bottom line is you need each of the seven in a high level to experience the super life. Otherwise the one failing area will start to drag the others down.

Takeaway: Your life has 7 areas.

What is Success To You?

Rate these on a scale from 0 – 10:

1. Family
2. Business
3. Physical Health
4. Spiritual
5. Financial
6. Communal
7. Recreational

To start the super life you have to get brutally honest with where you're at right now. Anything below a nine and you know you have some work to do.

Takeaway: Rating your different life areas is the first step on the route to fixing the places where you aren't having success.

"I WANT A MILLION DOLLARS IN MY HAPPY ACCOUNT AND A MILLION DOLLARS IN MY BANK ACCOUNT."

– Grant Cardone

10X SUPER LIFE

"Success doesn't happen to you, it happens because of you."

The 10X Super Life is up to you, it's your responsibility. Success will not come knock on your front door, you must go find it.

Takeaway: Make your dream life happen.

10X SUPER LIFE

THE PLAN

HOW TO CREATE YOUR SUPER LIFE

Get control of your life. You have a choice: feel good about yourself, or don't. *There really is no in between!* Your body, your appearance, your health, your goals, your planning, and your time are under your control.

10X SUPER LIFE

Commit Defined

- Pledge or bind to a certain course
- Be dedicated

Origin – join, entrust – put into custody

Commit: to pledge or bind (a person or an organization) to a certain course. But how does one commit so fully? The first step I take is to eliminate any and all other options and devote myself completely to learning everything I can about the topic. I become a fanatic. I am 100% absorbed, all-in, obsessed, a Super Freak! I stop questioning, planning, over-thinking and get in all the way.

I discontinue looking at other options. Don't be the guy who keeps looking in everyone else's lawn to see how the grass is greener "over there." That's the same guy who never commits to taking care of the lawn he already has. He just winds up mediocre and miserable. What was he even doing looking at another lawn in the first place?

Takeaway: Commit to your Super Life.

10X SUPER LIFE PLEDGE

I pledge to 10X my professional career.

I commit to take action at 10X levels daily to ensure I am reaching my full potential in my career. I will invest time and money in having my 10X Profession.

I pledge to 10X my family life.

I will invest time, money, resources and care with my family to ensure we have a 10X family life. I create time for my immediate and extended family to ensure that my family is best equipped for survival.

I pledge to 10X my income.

I will take all ethical actions necessary to 10X my income.
I commit to learn the skills necessary to ensure that I am able to reach my 10X income goals. I will no longer settle for income that just allows me to barely get by and will do whatever it takes to 10X my income.

I pledge to 10X my financial wealth.

I will study the wealthy and duplicate their successful actions for building wealth. I will invest time and money on those things that allow me to grow my income and value in the marketplace to ensure I increase my wealth.

What do you need to SURVIVE HARDSHIP

1. Commitment
2. Energy
3. Health
4. Like-Minded network
5. Resources
6. Reserves

Doing something every day displays a commitment. You eat every day. You take a shower every day. Anything worth doing is worth doing every day. Anything you're going to practice, practice it every day. Anything you're going to read about, read about it every day. Now, if you can't stick with it, maybe there's something wrong with it. Or maybe something there's something you don't understand. You need more than just commitment to survive hardship. You need to have energy and health with your body, the right people around you, and plenty of resources.

Takeaway: Surviving hardship takes a Super Life.

10X Income

1. Set 10X Targets
2. Reinforce the purpose
3. Make it real daily
4. Increase income today
5. Learn what you must
6. Surround yourself with like-minded people

Money Doesn't Sleep. Money doesn't know about clocks, schedules or holidays and you shouldn't either. Money loves people that have a great work ethic. When I was 26 years old I was in retail and the store I worked in closed at 7pm; most times you could find me there at 11pm making an extra sale. Never try to be the smartest or luckiest person; just make sure you outwork everyone.

Takeaway: Work and hustle if you want income.

Income Distribution

82.7% of all world income is earned
by less than 20% of the people.

10X Wealth

Omnipresence. You want to find the rubies, the diamonds and the gold? You must become omnipresent, widely or constantly encountered. Omnipresence is the concept of being everywhere in all places at the same time. Never before in the history of mankind has it been more possible and less expensive to become omnipresent.

Your brand, your name, your face, your message, your company, your future, everything. You're connected to everyone now. Either be used by it or use it. You want wealth, get known.

Takeaway: Get everywhere and be everywhere for wealth.

Omnipresence Defined

Widely or constantly encountered; conveys the concept of being everywhere in all places, at the same time.

In order for your life not to feel like "work" -- or like you're running on a hamster wheel -- you must think in terms of the right volumes. Omnipresence -- the goal of being everywhere at all times and at the same time -- is exactly the kind of massive thinking that is missing from most people's expectations of themselves and their dreams.

Can you imagine what it would be like if you, your brand, and your company could be everywhere all the time -- and how much power this would give you?

Takeaway: Omnipresence is massive think.

Omnipresence

Show me one great company that has not accomplished omnipresence. Coca-Cola, McDonald's, Google, Starbucks, AT&T, Bank of America, Apple, Ford Motor Company, Visa, American Express, Wal-Mart—these names are everywhere. Each of these companies is in every city—some on every street corner—and most are available around the world. You see their ads, you know what their logos look like, and you can even hum some of their jingles and use their names to describe not just their products; but in some cases, their competitors' products as well.

There are also individuals who have accomplished omnipresence so well that the world immediately recognizes their names, such as Steve Jobs, Oprah, Bill Gates, Warren Buffett, George Bush, Barack Obama, Abe Lincoln, Elvis, the Beatles, Led Zeppelin, Walt Disney, Will Smith, Mother Teresa, Muhammad Ali, Michael Jackson, Michael Jordan, and so on. Whether you like them or not, each of these people has created such a name for himself or herself that most people know who they are—or at the very least, recognize their name and align it with importance.

Takeaway: Get known and you'll be recognized with importance.

Wealth Graph

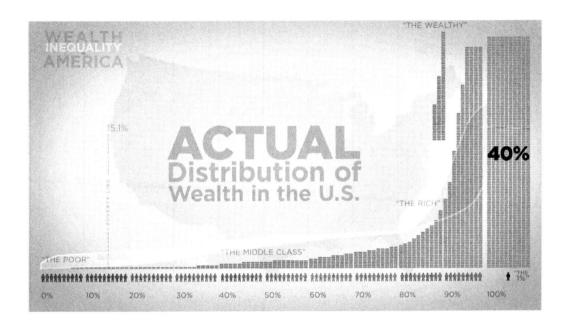

The lesson here is to get rich.

10X Health

1. Set 10X Targets
2. Daily ritual
3. Increase health today
4. What do you need to give up?
5. What do you need to learn?
6. Surround yourself with like-minded people

No matter what area of life, the steps remain the same. Memorize these.

Takeaway: No matter what area, the basic building blocks to 10X your life are similar.

10X Family

1. Set 10X Targets
2. Daily rituals
3. Increase family interaction
4. What do you need to give up?
5. What do you need to learn?
6. Surround yourself with like-minded people.

Everyone wants to have a great family life. And I am not just talking about your personal success, but the success of your children, your marriage, your immediate and extended family, your company and its survival, even your generation, and our great country. Take a minute and see that all your actions affect those around you in ever widening circles. When you get yourself into action and achieve your goals, you are not the only person that benefits.

Takeaway: A great family will impact future generations.

10X Spiritual Life

1. Set 10X Targets

2. Daily ritual making it real

3. Increase spiritual condition

4. What do you need to give up?

5. What do you need to learn?

6. Surround yourself with like-minded people.

Anything you don't take massive amounts of action in will subside and eventually cease to exist.

Takeaway: Spiritually, if you're not growing, you're contracting.

10X Recreational Life

1. Set 10X Targets
2. Daily ritual making it real
3. Increase your playtime
4. What do you need to give up?
5. What do you need to learn?
6. Surround yourself with like-minded people.

You get what you focus on. Whatever you have focused on has happened to you. This has already taken place in your life so I'm not asking you to do anything different. What you're focusing on right now is what you're getting. No person is happy without a goal. People must have faith in the ability to reach a goal in order to be happy. Without goals, hopes, ambitions—without the attainment of pleasure it is nearly impossible to be happy. My goals bring me pleasure. Security lies in the confidence a person has to reach their goals. Get serious about your recreational life.

Takeaway: If you want fun, get serious.

"YOU ARE GUARANTEED SUCCESS AT CREATING A SUPER LIFE IF YOU MERELY REFUSE TO QUIT."

– Grant Cardone

10X SUPER LIFE

COMMIT EVERYTHING YOU HAVE TO CREATING A SUPER LIFE

- YOUR MONEY
- YOUR ENERGY
- YOUR FEARS
- YOUR HOME
- YOUR JOB
- YOUR EXCUSES

Do you know where you are going? Do you have that look in your eye? Are those around you clear that you are on a mission? Have you made it known that you are unstoppable? Do others notice this intense look on your face and in your posture?

When you become intently focused on where you are going it will change the look on your face, in your eye, your posture and your voice. When you become determined, committed, dedicated, and obsessed, others will know you are, and treat you accordingly.

Takeaway: Commitment will change you.

Give Up Bad Habits

- BAD HABITS
- PORNOGRAPHY
- DRUGS
- ALCOHOL
- VIDEO GAMES
- OLD FRIENDS
- CLUBBING
- TV
- WASTING TIME

- NEGATIVITY
- BITCHING
- FAMILY
- MONEY
- COMFORT
- FREE TIME
- LAZINESS
- LATE NIGHTS

10X SUPER LIFE

Run for your life from Middle Class

- Comfort
- Conventional
- Comparison
- Settle
- Passive
- Security

Driven, destined, focused, committed, obsessed and no longer distracted by obstacles of normal people is the beingness of the most successful. The most successful make it clear they will not be distracted by the temptations that distract the normals.

Takeaway: The Middle Class is full of normal.

Reasons the Middle Class is Failing

1. Brainwashed
2. Unwilling to confront reality
3. Not in Control of Income
4. Spends rather than Invests
5. Goals Too Small
6. Settles

Adopt the beingness of the most successful so that no one will dare tempt you or try to distract you. Take on the posture of those that made it all the way. When you make a complete commitment to success all will know it.

When it happened to me old friends would often say, "You're so serious," "You're no fun anymore," and "Can't you just enjoy life?" If you aren't hearing your friends say this to you, well then... you can still be distracted. The very same people that were disappointed with me years ago, now say, "I always knew you were going to be successful."

Takeaway: People who criticize you today will praise you in the future.

Never Underestimate Reality

What is the Cause of the Failing

1. Wrong Think
2. Wrong Goals
3. Incorrect Levels of Action

When I first started playing with social media I posted twice a day. I don't know what I was thinking—it was a moment of "little think." We simultaneously began sending out e-mail strategies once a month and found ourselves getting requests from people who wanted to be removed from our e-mail campaign. My colleagues suggested I back off. That is when I woke up and came to my senses. Get rid of your wrong think. Launch into orbit, never fly under the radar.

Takeaway: Wrong levels of action cause failure.

Wrong Think Defined

1. Comfort not **Freedom**
2. Jobs not **Careers**
3. Income not **Wealth**
4. Spend Money vs **Invest Money**
5. Options vs **Mandatory**
6. $50k vs **$500k**
7. Or vs **Both**

Examples of wrong thinking:

Don't talk to strangers. If you're not talking to strangers, you aren't going any place in your life. You aren't going to venture out into the world. Opportunity doesn't just knock once.

You can't have your cake and eat it to. Why the hell do you have cake then?

Four Biggest Mistakes in Goal Setting

1. Too Small a Goal
2. Too Narrow a Goal
3. Someone Else's Goals
4. Comparison Goals

Successful people dream big and have immense goals. They are not "realistic." They leave that to the masses who fight for leftovers. The middle class is taught to be realistic and average, whereas the successful think in terms of how extensively they can spread themselves. It's not about being average. It's about being above average. The greatest regret of my life is that I initially set targets and goals based on what was realistic rather than on giant, radical thinking.

Takeaway: Realistic think leads to failure.

Four Degrees of Action Determine the Outcome of Your Goals

1. Do Nothing
2. Retreat as an action
3. **Normal (middle) levels of action**
4. Massive action

When you start operating at the fourth degree of action, your mind-set will shift and so will your results. You will end up instigating opportunities that you will have to address earlier, later, and in a different way than you would on a "normal" day, so a routine day will become a thing of the past. I continued this commitment to massive action until one day it was no longer an unusual activity but a habit for me. It was interesting to see how many people would ask me, "Why are you still out this late?" "What are you doing calling on a Saturday?" "You never quit, do you?" " I wish my people worked like this." And even —"What are you on?"

Takeaway: Living massive will get you noticed.

Set New Financial Targets

1. 10X Income
2. 10X Savings
3. 10X Investments
4. 10X Retirement
5. 10X Net Worth

Have daily targets. Just like you have a lifetime target, a monthly target, an annual target, have some daily targets. What do you want to accomplish today? What do you want to hit today? Who do you want to contact today? What would be a successful day? Did I wake up on time? Did I go to sleep early? Did I spend time with the family? Did I spend time with the kids? Did I get my workout in? What's your daily target? Get specific with your financial goals.

Takeaway: New targets are a must if you want to achieve higher levels.

Commitment to Goals

1. Never Lower Your Target or a Goal
2. Increase the Activity to Acquire the Goal
3. Write goals Daily
4. Get the Family Involved
5. Be Unreasonable

I want to see what I am accomplishing. Why? It's fuel! It makes me feel good about myself rather than focusing on the losses and the failures and I didn't do this and I didn't do that. I want to stay focused on my daily target. Now write down your daily target. What are you focused on today? What would make it a great day? What do you have to see happen today that would make it a target worth achieving and make you feel good about yourself?

Takeaway: Give yourself fuel.

Goals / Target Attainment

1. The target is never the problem.
2. Any target attacked with the right amount and persistence of actions is attainable.

The only way to get through life is to sell. John Kennedy, master orator and salesperson knew it and sold America on landing man to the moon. Martin Luther King understood the need to sell with his Dream Speech. Obama knows the value of selling, watch his victory speech. They all had targets and attained them. Every goal you have must be a target that you can attack.

Takeaway: Attack your targets like a hungry dog.

Assume Control of Everything

NOTHING HAPPENS TO YOU, IT HAPPENS BECAUSE OF YOU.

You must understand—as I've already stated countless times—that success is not something that happens *to* you; it's something that happens *because* of you and because of the actions you take. People who refuse to take responsibility generally don't do well at taking much action and subsequently don't do well in the game of success. Successful people accept very high levels of accountability for creating and having success for themselves—and even for failing to do so. Successful people hate the blame game and know that it is better to make something happen—good *or* bad—than to have it happen to you.

Takeaway: You are in control.

Victims Assume No Control

1. Bad things happen to them
2. Bad things happen to them often
3. They are always involved
4. **Someone or something else is always to blame**

Let's say that someone rear-ends me. Clearly, that person is at fault. Although I will be upset with him or her, the last thing I want to do is assume the position of victim. How horrible! "Look what happened to me – oh, poor me, I am a victim." Would you get a business card or have a television campaign state this to the public as a way to garner respect and attention? Of course not! Never claim the position of victim after deciding to create a life filled with success. Instead, figure out how to reduce the chances of inconveniences, like people rear-ending you, from ever happening again. In order to make good things happen more often, you cannot afford to act like a victim.

Takeaway: You are not a victim.

Average is an Epidemic

Webster's dictionary defines average as: "a level that is typical of a group, class, or series : a middle point between extremes." Who want's that? If you're in a race, where do you want to be? Not in the middle. The word average can be traced back to the fifteenth century. Some of this word was used in the Arabic language and it meant "damaged merchandise." Are you damaged merchandise? No human being should ever be considered damaged merchandise!

Takeaway: Average Sucks

How Do You Know You Are Taking Massive Action

1. You will get a new set of problems
2. Immediately see your weaknesses
3. Get criticized
4. Your competition will start promoting you

Takeaway: When you are taking massive action, you aren't thinking of terms of how many hours you work.

"One Day I'm going to make it until then I'll just keep hustling."
– Grant Cardone

10X SUPER LIFE

10X Lifestyle vs. Average Lifestyle

Unreasonable	Reasonable
Obsessed	Never Commits
Fearless	Fearful
All-In	Safe Bets
Labeled	Fits In
Never Satisfied	Complacent
Expanding	Contracting
Only Way	No Way
Freedom Seeking	Comfort Seeking

"You can't get rich thinking poor"

10X SUPER LIFE

Rich vs. Poor

Success is Obligation	Success is Evil
Invest Money	Spend Money
Uses Debt for Investments	Uses Debt for Spending
Thinks with "both"	Thinks with "one or the other"
Has Financial Plan	Has a Budget
Expands	Contracts
Makes things happen	Things happen to them
Reads and Studies	Refuses to Study
Responsible	Blames others
Attention on the Future	Attention on the Past
Thinks in Solutions	Thinks in Problems
Buys Time	Wastes Time
Multiple Flows of Income	Single Flow
Net Worth Driven	Income Driven
Pays Self First	Pays Others First
Goal Driven	Work Driven

"You can't get rich thinking poor"

10X Challenges

Do those things that challenge you the most! Quit doing the things that don't challenge you. Look, you've got to get challenged. I don't care what it is; jump out of a plane, jump off of a bridge, go ask somebody out that you know won't go out with you, go call Donald Trump's office... do something that challenges you! Run for mayor, do anything that pushes you or challenges you or puts you into a different realm and I guarantee you, your experience is probably going to be a bit of anxiety, maybe some fear but underneath that there is always motivation.

Maybe make a list of things that would most challenge you. For instance, when I am making sales calls, I don't make the easiest ones first. I make the most difficult ones first. I want to get those ones that challenge me the most out of my way or I want to conquer them. Either way I win. If I make the hardest call first and I win. I am on fire baby! Particularly when I put the other 99 tips together of how to stay motivated. Now, if I make that most difficult call and I lose, at least it is out of the way – it's a no-brainer. Most people take the easiest things first. They're not challenging themselves that's why they're not motivated.

"When you are taking massive action, you aren't thinking of terms of how many hours you work"

Takeaway: Challenge yourself.

10X Challenges

People are setting targets too low and doing simple, easy things everyday. I try to 10X everything; I try to find the best parking space everywhere I go. My wife is like, "What are you doing going around and around?" I am going to get a good spot.

I guarantee you that I am going to get a good spot. I don't need to settle for a bad spot, I might even park in a place that says, "Don't Park Here" because I want that good spot.

Do the things that challenge you the most. Don't break the law, don't do things that are unethical but push yourself, challenge yourself and do the things that push you the most!

Takeaway: When you are taking massive action, you aren't thinking of terms of how many hours you work.

Start 10X'ing Your Life

- Set Goals at 10X Levels
- Get into the right amount of action
- Keep taking massive action
- Get Criticism
- Get Haters
- Get Admiration
- Immerse Yourself in 10X
- Succeed at All Cost

The idea of being overwhelmed by challenges, I believe, is the result of two things: Never taking enough action to generate the experience of overcoming challenges or a lack of SKILLS necessary to provide confidence in the resolution of challenges.

Takeaway: Get skills.

The 10X Rule is the Holy Grail for those who desire the Super Life

Success begets more success, and experiencing losses increase your chances of more losses. Challenges are the experiences that sharpen successful people's abilities. To achieve your goals, you have to get to a place where every challenge becomes fuel for you. Life can be quite brutal, and people can incur a fair amount of losses over time. Many get to a point where every new challenge they face automatically equals a loss in their mind. You must use the 10X Rule in your life.

Takeaway: Challenges sharpen you.

No Shortage of Success

Unlike a product that is manufactured and inventoried, there is no "limit" as to how much success can be created.

"Laziness" is an entitlement concept accepted by the middle class that's crushing America's greatness and spreading like a cancer. Laziness is the 'new' adopted "right" of people, supposedly earned because a person worked five days and therefore must take the weekend off. This concept of entitlement runs across workers, management and executives across the country. To have success you must get rid of all laziness, and then you'll realize there is no shortage of success, there's just an abundance of laziness going around!

Takeaway: Laziness will always limit success.

I Commit to a Super Life

- Family   10X
- Business   10X
- Health   10X
- Spiritual   10X
- Financial   10X
- Community   10X
- Recreation   10X

Make your commitment today. Everything starts with a commitment—a marriage, a business, a fitness program—whatever it is you must commit to have success.

Takeaway: Commit today.

Study The Super Successful

- Commitment to success
- Invest in success (expansion)
- Invest in Education
- Invest in Like-Minded people
- Trade money for Time
- Connect with Power
- Surpluses

Because I never trusted my talents, my looks or my luck, and I had no connections, I studied what successful people did and tried to mimic that. Then I studied what unsuccessful people did and tried to avoid that. While there are many things that seem to differentiate those who are successful from those who aren't, I've noticed one simple difference that stands out the most—successful people are often more willing.

Takeaway: Study the successful.

Run for your life

- 46% of all workers fear they don't have enough money to retire.
- 57% of all workers have less than $10k in retirement savings.
- Poverty population is growing in America.
- 46 million people are on food stamps.
- 50% of college educated people can't get work in their field.
- 2/3 of all businesses break even or lose money.
- 75% of all small businesses have zero employees.

Takeaway: Don't be a statistic. In order to have a super life you must do what others refuse to do.

"I AM DONE LIVING IN FEAR WITH THE LIES OF SOCIETY THAT HAVE ME SETTLING FOR CRUMBS AND LEFTOVERS."

– Grant Cardone

10X SUPER LIFE

Questions:
10X Super Life

1. What level of action is the most dangerous, because it is accepted by society as enough?

2. The more attention you get the more _____ you can make.

3. There is a shortage of money on this planet. True / False

4. They say the number one reason people go bankrupt is because of health problems. True / False

5. How would you define extraordinary?

No Motivation, No Super Life

A lack of motivation is a main reason people don't have the 10X Super Life power to make their goals a reality. Look, like my daddy told me, "if you run out of gas, you ain't going to make your destination." Success requires a particular 'gas', called motivation. Most people lack the proper amounts and then believe they lack the ability to produce more motivation on their own accord. Walking on fire, with my friend, Tony Robbins will give you an immediate pump but you must learn the skill of creating, managing and regenerating motivation at will, especially through failures. There are exact strat egies that I have practiced to get me through hundreds of fa ilures over the last 30 years. You must have the right degree of motivation/desire to make your goals a reality.

Course 9

To get rich you need to flip that switch to ignite your fire and get moving toward your dreams. Everyone needs to be fired up from time to time. Use this to get your mojo on, get jacked, and stay highly energetic. A motivated person gets stuff done. Stay motivated 365 days a year and you will be more productive than anyone you know.

100 Ways to Stay Motivated Exercises:

1. Approach Success as Your Duty, Not an Option
- Make a list of at least five things you have to be successful in. (Business, personal, etc.)
- Success is it not an option, but a duty. Are you are successful in these areas?

2. Approach Success as an Ethical Issue, Not a Financial One
- Write a short essay on how being successful ties in with your personal moral code.
- After seeing how being successful ties in with your ethics, how do you feel about going after your target goals?

3. Be the Most Ethical Person You Know
- List ways, besides being honest, you can become the most ethical person you know.
- Write how you can implement this in your life.

4. Be the Most Professionally Dressed Person in Your Space
- Go to your closet and put together at least 3 professional outfits.
- Why is it that being dressed professionally is important not only to others, but to yourself?

5. Be the Most Dependable Person You Know
- Make a list of 10 ways you can be dependable and implement them today. What Happened?

6. Let People Know You Are Unique By Your Actions
- Write down 5 actions you can take that are unique to you and would differentiate you from others.

100 Ways to Stay Motivated Exercises:

7. Go to Bed Early
- Tonight go to bed an hour earlier than you usually do. Tomorrow, write what you noticed about your production and energy compared to the previous day.

8. Be the First One up in your Neighborhood
- Tomorrow, set your alarm one hour earlier than usual and force yourself out of bed. See how much more did you got done .

9. Stay So Busy You Run Everywhere you Go
- Why is it you won't burn out running from event to event but you will burn out when you do nothing? Give an example.
- How can you ensure you stay so busy you have to run everywhere you go?

10. Do Those things that Challenge You the Most
- Make a list of things that would most challenge you and do at least one today. How did you feel afterwards?

11. Do Those Things You are Fearful of
- Make a list of 5 things you are fearful of doing then complete one of them today.
- How did you feel after you did it?

12. Eat the Healthiest Foods You Can Afford
- Make a list of the foods you are eating that you KNOW are not good for you. Eliminate one of them today from your diet.
- What was your energy level like after you did not eat that food for today?

13. Avoid Foods with Sugars
- For one day, avoid all foods with sugar. Write down the result.

100 Ways to Stay Motivated Exercises:

14. Increase Water Intake
- How much water do you consume every day? Today, drink two 8 oz. glasses more than you usually do. What happened?

15. Be Energetic Even When You Don't Feel It
- Take an opportunity at some point today to take action or get involved, even if you "aren't feeling it" or "are lagging." What happened?

16. Overcommit to your Family and Clients
- Write at least 5 ways you can overcommit AND over-deliver to your family and clients.

17. Say Yes to Life
- Write down at least 3 things (ethical and pro survival) that you have been saying "No" to and just say "Yes." What happened once you started doing this?

18. Give More than is Expected of You
- Make a list of 3 simple ways you can give more than is expected of you.
- Do what you wrote down for your list. What happened?

19. Show up Early for Everything
- Show up early for your appointments, work, etc. What happened when you showed up early?

20. Make a List of Contacts that Would Change your Life
- Before you go to sleep tonight, make a list of at least 5 people that, if you contacted them it would change your life. What would be the first step in making contact with one of them?

100 Ways to Stay Motivated Exercises:

21. Work to Your Potential Not Your Quota
- Write down what your potential is and compare it to a current "quota" in your life. How does it compare?

22. Get in a Mastermind Group of Winners
- Make a list of your 5 closest friends and write what you have in common with them. Are all of these similarities optimal?
- Now find of a mastermind group of winners in your field of interest or business and join it.

23. Read a Book a Week.
- Make a list of three books you are interested in reading.
- Choose one and read it this week. (If it takes you less time, great! Get another and start reading it.)

24. Look to Control Time rather than Manage It
- What are 3 ways you can CONTROL time rather than MANAGE it?

25. Schedule Your Day in 15- Minute Blocks
- Make a schedule for your day cramming as much as you can into 15 minute blocks then adhere to it for one day. What happened?

26. Get Great Partners
- Make a list of qualities that would be necessary in great partners in any aspect of life.

27. Cut Out Negative People
- Make a list of all the people who you are frequently in contact with in your life and determine if they are positive or negative. What occurs when you are in contact with the negative people?

100 Ways to Stay Motivated Exercises:

28. Be Deaf When Someone Says you Can't
- For one day, be deaf to all negativity around you. What happened? How did you feel?

29. Be Honest with Everyone Especially Yourself
- Be Honest with yourself and write the answers to the following questions:
    - a) What is your potential?
    - b) How much can you do in one week?
    - c) One day?
    - d) One hour?
    - e) 15 minutes?
    - f) What do you need to do to provide for yourself and your family?

30. Exercise a Little Everyday
- Exercise for 30 minutes today. How did you feel afterward?
- Write in your own words your own commitment to exercise a little every day.

31. Make Quality Time for Your Family Everyday
- On your calendar, block off quality time to spend with each member of your family each day.

32. Have a higher purpose than Just Money.
- Find your higher purpose than just money. What do you want money for? Write down your answer.

33. Shoot for Extraordinary
- Write down 5 extraordinary goals for yourself in business and in life.

100 Ways to Stay Motivated Exercises:

34. Keep Statistics on Everything Important
- Make a list of everything that is important to your success and find a way to keep statistics on each.
- Keep a graph on all of the above for a week. What happened?

35. Dominate Your Space Don't Compete in It
- How can you dominate your space?

36. Get So Much Attention You Are Criticized For It
- Write 3 ways you can get more attention. What can you expect when more attention is coming to you?

37. Make the News Don't Watch the News
- Write down three ways you can make the news in your area or be newsworthy.

38. Become a Celebrity in Your Space
- Write, in your own words, your decision to become a celebrity in your space and how you will do so.

39. Keep a Full Calendar
- Fill up your calendar for the next week with events and activities.

40. Never Settle For Good when You Can Be Great
- Write an example of something you strived to be great at. How did you do?
- Write down a time when you know you settled for less than your potential. What decisions have you made with regard to this?

100 Ways to Stay Motivated Exercises:

41. Do a Little More than the Day Before
- Review what you did yesterday and do one or two more things today than yesterday. What happened when you did that?

42. Be a Maniac at Your Life and Your Career
- Make a list of at least 3 ways that you can be a maniac in your personal life and in the workplace.

43. Do so Much You Are Criticized for It
- Choose an activity today and keep doing it to the point you are criticized for it. What occurred while doing this?

44. Take Everything You Do to Another Level
- Write an example of how you can take something you are doing now to another level.

45. Write Your Goals Down First Thing Each Day
- Get a note pad or start a document in your computer and for three days write down your goals first thing each day.
- Write down what happened in those three days.

46. Write Your Goals down Again Before You Go to Sleep
- Now, for three more days, as well as writing your goals down when you first wake up, write them before you go to sleep.
- Write down what happened in those three days.

47. Have a 30 Minute Finance Meeting with Your Family
- This week have a 30 minute financial meeting with your family.
- What happened? What did you find out?

100 Ways to Stay Motivated Exercises:

48. Have a Monthly Goals Meeting with Your Family
- Have a monthly goals meeting with your family.
- What occurred when you did this? How do you feel about your goals and those of your family?

49. Reach Up for New Friends
- Write down things you could do, places you could go, etc. where you could reach up for new friends.
- Choose a couple of these actions and do them.

50. Ask Those More Successful Than You for Guidance
- Identify one or two people more successful than you that you can go to for guidance and get some advice.
- Arrange to meet or speak to them for guidance.

51. Stay Involved with Your Community-Be Social
- Write down 3 ways you could become more involved with your community.
- Choose one and do it this week. What happened?

52. Stay Uncomfortable and Meet New People
- In a group of people, or just out in public, introduce yourself to 3 people you are uncomfortable or tentative to approach. What occurred?

53. Get Some Big New Juicy Problems Rather than Old Boring One's
- Write down at least 5 examples of big new juicy problems that would really freak you out.

100 Ways to Stay Motivated Exercises:

54. Be the Most Positive person You Know
- Today be the most positive person in your environment. What Happened? How did people react to you?

55. Surround Yourself with Positive Reminders
- Put some positive reminders in your space. Note anything you observed as a result of this.

56. Go the Extra mile Even After you have Satisfied your requirement.
- When doing an activity today, go the extra mile. How did YOU feel after doing it?

57. Be so Big in Your Space Everyone is Talking About You
- Write at least three examples of how you can become a giant in your space.

58. Do What Others Refuse to Do
- Make a list of what others around you are unwilling to do.
- Choose one of these actions and do it today. What Happened when you did it?

59. Be Willing to Fail Knowing Failure is Impossible
- Write in your own words how you must be willing to fail because actual failure is not truly possible.

60. Write a Daily Battle Plan
- Write a battle plan for today then complete all the tasks you have laid out.
- What happened afterward?

100 Ways to Stay Motivated Exercises:

61. Stay Focused on the Daily Target
- – Write down your daily target for today.
- – What happened during the day with a target to focus on?

62. Do the Most Difficult Things First
- – Write your battle plan for today. Look over your list and identify your most difficult tasks and do them first.
- – How did you feel at the end of the day?

63. Take Enough Time Off to Fulfill Your Desire for Time Off
- – Write down what would be enough time to fulfill your desire for time off and why that would be enough time.

64. Go to Workshops to Learn and Connect
- – Make a list of three workshops that would be ideal for you to learn and connect at and work out how you can get yourself there.

65. Get Out of the House and Try New Things
- – This week get out of the house and try something new. Write down what happened. Was it good, bad, interesting?

66. Avoid Ads that Promote Depression as a Disease
- – For two days avoid ads that promote depression as a disease. What happened as a result?

67. Avoid Drama TV and Radio
- – For another two days avoid drama TV and radio. Did you feel more or less productive?

100 Ways to Stay Motivated Exercises:

68. Have Rewards for Accomplishments that Compliment Your Potential
  - Make a list of 5 rewards for accomplishments that are congruent with your actual potential.

69. Never Lower Your Target Mentality
  - Make a list of unreasonable targets and go for accomplishing them this week. Do not lower them.
  - What happened after going for these targets this week?

70. Schedule Short Breaks
  - Schedule four short breaks throughout your day today. How did it affect you?

71. Take Power naps if They Help You
  - Try taking a power nap today. Did it help you?

72. Picture What You Want at the End of the Deal
  - Picture what you want to accomplish at the END of your next deal. Write it down. Then go about the rest of the steps to accomplishing it. What Happened?

73. Keep Images of What It is you Want in Your Environment
  - Collect some images you want in the future. Post them up in your space.

74. Stay Around Hitters and Winners
  - Identify at least three hitters and winners in your life and work out how you can get yourself around them more often.

100 Ways to Stay Motivated Exercises:

75. Avoid those That Don't Assume Responsibility for Every Outcome
- Make a list of those in your life that don't assume responsibility for every outcome.
- For three days, avoid these people. How did that affect you?

76. Move with Speed and Urgency on Every Task
- Write down why Grant advises to move with speed and urgency on every task.

77. Stay hungry and Act hungry with Every person You Meet
- Act hungry with one person you meet today. What occurred?

78. Never Compromise your Potential for Being Satisfied
- Write down, in your own words, your own commitment to never compromise your potential for being satisfied and how you will avoid compromise.

79. Look at How things are possible Rather than Impossible
- Write down a task in your life that you consider impossible. Now write down at least 3 ways it could be possible.

80. Look to Accomplish Those things Others Say Can't be Done
- Make a list of 2 tasks that others around you say cannot be done.
- Today, put them on your to-do list. What happened?

81. Listen to Music that Pumps You Up
- Ten minutes before work, listen to some of your favorite music. What affect did this create on you?

100 Ways to Stay Motivated Exercises:

82. Cut Out All Behavior that lowers Your Self Esteem
- Make a list of all behaviors that lower your self-esteem.
- For 3 days cease all of the behaviors you listed. What happened when you did this?

83. Create Daily Rituals That Put You in Charge
- Create some daily rituals that put you in charge and implement them tomorrow. How did you do throughout the day?

84. Push Yourself to Do More than You Think is Possible
- Write at least 3 examples of ways you can push yourself to do more than you think is possible. Do you need someone else to help you? If so, identify that person.

85. Identify What You Are passionate About
- Make a list of the things you are truly passionate about.

86. Visit Your Customers in Person
- Meet at least 2 customers, clients, potential employers, etc. in person today. Write down what happened.

87. Write Down the Successes You Are Having
- Make a list of the successes in your life right now.
- What was the result of doing this exercise?

88. Call Every problem Customer Personally and Quickly
- Make a list of every problem contact in your life right now; then call them all as quickly as possible to resolve the issues. What happened?

100 Ways to Stay Motivated Exercises:

89. Get Things Done Long Before Required of You
- Get something done today way earlier than is expected. What Occurred when you did this?

90. Bring More to a Presentation than You Could Ever Use
- Write an example of how you could bring more to your next presentation than you could ever use and how this would be advantageous.

91. Complete Every Task Once Started
- Every task you start today, finish it. Write down what happened.

92. Focus on the Future not the Past
- Write down three examples of how you can get yourself out of the past or present and into the future.

93. Respond to All Social Media Likes and Comments
- Today respond to all communication you receive. (Facebook, phone calls, e-mails, etc.) What occurred when you did this?

94. Make Sure the Whole World Knows You
- Write down three ways you can make sure the whole world knows you.

95. Make Continued and Regular Investments in Yourself
- Make a list of 3 ways you can make regular and continued investments in yourself.

96. Seek to be Exceptional in Every Area of Your Life
- Write down what exactly it would mean for you to be exceptional in every area of your life.

100 Ways to Stay Motivated Exercises:

97. Break Your life into Priorities and Win at All of them
  - Write down all your priorities in life. Then, going down the list, mark them on a scale of 1-10 of how well you are doing with them.
  - In your own words, write your own commitment to get to a 10 rating on all these priorities.

98. Everyday Look for Opportunity to Help others
  - Help someone out today. Write down what happened when you did this.

99. Stay in the BEST Hotels
  - Write down in your own words why you should stay at the best hotels you can.

100. Fly First Class
  - Write down the advantages to flying first class.

101. Never Never Never Compare Yourself to Money
  - Write down all the ways in which you are more valuable than money.

Author: G Cardone
Author: Grant Cardone

Printed in Great Britain
by Amazon

32504149R00236